Life and Religion

An Aftermath from the Writings of the
Right Honourable Professor
F. MAX MÜLLER

**COMPILED AND ARRANGED
BY HIS WIFE, GEORGINA**

THE BOOK TREE
Glendale, California

First printed by Doubleday, Page & Co., 1905
© 1995 THE BOOK TREE

Second Edition

ISBN 1-885395-10-8

Printed in the United States of America

THE BOOK TREE
P.O. Box 5446
Glendale, CA 91221

THE BOOK TREE

INTRODUCTION

Max Muller was quite likely the closest one can get to being the ideal religious scholar. His accomplishments were many, including translating the Upanishads and writing a massive work on Eastern religions. He praised Jesus highly, as well, from the perspective of Western religion. He was a true expert in all religious areas. Simply put, Muller was regarded as the greatest religious scholar of his time.

Yet Muller had something more than a keen scholarly and analytical mind. He had warmth, and emotion. He knew how to touch the human soul with his writings, and to bring people closer to their spiritual essence.

This is a collection of his deepest, most meaningful quotes. This book reflects the true wisdom of a man who understood the human spirit. These are his *personal* thoughts, many not found in his more scholarly works. They compose a book that simply can not be read from cover to cover like a novel. A few pages at a time work best because one must pause to digest them, and absorb their meaning.

You come across very few books in your lifetime that are jam-packed with incredible wisdom and have the potential to move you in such a powerful way that it changes your thinking forever. This is one of those books. It qualifies, if you do. You must be capable of reflecting deeply on his words, to understand them, to have a sense of wonder, and compassion. If you have a sense as to what your spirit or soul might be, and can relate to it at least part of the time, then this book will touch you like no other.

If, however, you have no interest in spiritual or religious matters, this book is not for you. People enmeshed in the material world will have no idea what Muller is talking about. Nor will they care. And that is a shame because it is only through wisdom like this, and its understanding, that the world will change for the better. Mankind still has many lessons to learn. That is why we are here. If enough of us realize this fact, humble ourselves, and explore the human soul, we can make progress together no matter where we are from. If used appropriately, this book is a great place to start.

Rev. Paul Tice

PREFACE

THIS book has been prepared in accordance with a wish expressed by many known and unknown admirers of my husband's writings who desire to possess in portable form the various striking passages in his different works and in the "Life and Letters" that have specially appealed to them.

I have taken the opportunity of adding extracts from many private letters, and from the writings he left unfinished—passages that would otherwise have remained unknown to any but his own family and a few intimate friends.

Those who have read the "Life and Letters" do not need to be told that Max Müller entertained from his earliest years the firm conviction that all is wisely ordered in this life, "all for our real good, though we do not always see it, and though we cannot venture to fathom the wisdom guiding our steps." To other readers the unswerving trust and faith shown in these extracts may be a revelation, for he rarely conversed on such subjects. Yet this trust and faith gave him strength through the bitter struggles of his early life, taught

v

him resignation during the years when the dearest wish of his heart seemed unattainable, supported him later when those whom he loved tenderly were taken from him, and upheld him in his long and depressing illness.

It is my earnest desire that this little book may prove a help and comfort to those who endure like trials, and that it may strengthen those whose path in life now stretches before them, filled with sunshine, to meet the sorrows that inevitably await us all.

GEORGINA MAX MÜLLER.

June 11, 1905.

CONTENTS

vii

CONTENTS—*Continued*

LIFE AND RELIGION

THE ART OF LIFE

To learn to understand one another is the great art of life, and to "agree to differ" is the best lesson of the comparative science of religion.

Silesian Horseherd.

There is a higher kind of music which we all have to learn, if our life is to be harmonious, beautiful, and useful. There are certain intervals between the young and the old which must be there, which are meant to be there, without which life would be monotonous; but out of these intervals and varieties, the true art of life knows how to build up perfect harmonies. . . . Even great sorrow may be a blessing, by drawing some of our affections away from this life to a better life . . . of which, it is true, we know nothing, but from which, when we see the wisdom and love that underlie this life, we may hope everything. We are meant to hope and to trust, and that is often much harder than to see, and to know. . . . The greatest of all arts is the art of life, and the best of all music the harmony of spirits.

3

There are many little rules to be learnt for giving harmony and melody to our life, but the thorough bass must be—love.   *Life.*

One thing is necessary above all things in order to live peaceably with people; that is, in Latin, *Humanitas*, German, *Menschlichkeit.* It is difficult to describe, but it is to claim as little as possible from others, neither an obliging temper nor gratitude, and yet to do all one can to please others, yet without expecting them always to find it out. As men are made up of contradictions, they are the more grateful and friendly the less they see that we expect gratitude and friendliness. Even the least cultivated people have their good points, and it is not only far better but far more interesting if one takes trouble to find out the best side and motives of people, rather than the worst and most selfish. . . . Life is an art, and more difficult than Sanscrit or anything else.
                                                Ibid.

We become chiefly what we are more through others than through ourselves, and happy is the man whose path in life leads him only by good men, and brings him together with good men. How often we forget in judging others the influences under which they have grown up. How can one expect a child to be truthful when he sees how servants, yes, often parents, practise deceit. How many children hear from those to whom they look up, expressions, principles, and prudent rules of life, which consciously or unconsciously exercise an influence on the young life of the child. Yet with how little of loving introspection we pass our judgments. *MS.*

If you want to be at peace with yourself, do not mind being at war with the world. *MS.*

THE BEAUTIFUL

Is the Beautiful without us, or is it not rather within us? What we call sweet and bitter is our own sweetness, our own bitterness, for nothing can be sweet or bitter without us. Is it not the same with the Beautiful? The world is like a rich mine, full of precious ore, but each man has to assay the ore for himself, before he knows what is gold, and what is not. What then is the touchstone by which we assay the Beautiful? We have a touchstone for discovering the good. Whatever is unselfish is good. But—though nothing can be beautiful, except what is, in some sense or other, good, not everything that is good is also beautiful. What, then, is that something which, added to the good, makes it beautiful? It is a great mystery. It is so to us as it was to Plato. We must have gazed on the Beautiful in the dreams of childhood, or, it may be, in a former life, and now we look for it everywhere, but we can never find it—never at least in all its brightness and fulness again, never as we remember it once as the vision of a half-forgotten dream. Nor do we all remember the same ideal—some

6

poor creatures remember none at all. . . .
The ideal, therefore, of what is beautiful is within
us, that is all we know; how it came there we shall
never know.   It is certainly not of this life, else
we could define it; but it underlies this life, else
we could not feel it.   Sometimes it meets us like
a smile of Nature, sometimes like a glance of God;
and if anything proves that there is a great past,
and a great future, a Beyond, a higher world, a
hidden life, it is our faith in the Beautiful.

Chips from a German Workshop.

THE BIBLE

THE fault is ours, not theirs, if we wilfully misinterpret the language of ancient prophets, if we persist in understanding their words in their outward and material aspect only, and forget that before language had sanctioned a distinction between the concrete and the abstract, between the purely spiritual as opposed to the coarsely material, the intention of the speakers comprehended both the concrete and the abstract, both the material and the spiritual, in a manner which has become quite strange to us, though it lives on in the language of every true poet.

Science of Religion.

Canonical books give the reflected image only of the real doctrines of the founder of a new religion; an image always blurred and distorted by the medium through which it had to pass.

Ibid.

The Old Testament stands on a higher ethical stage than other sacred books—it certainly does not lose by a comparison with them. I always said so, but people would not believe it. Still, anything to show the truly historical and human character of the Old Testament would be extremely useful in any sense, and would in no wise injure the high character which it possesses.

Life.

If we have once learned to be charitable and reasonable in the interpretation of the sacred books of other religions, we shall more easily learn to be charitable and reasonable in the interpretation of our own. We shall no longer try to force a literal sense on words which, if interpreted literally, must lose their true and original purport; we shall no longer interpret the Law and the Prophets as if they had been written in the English of our own century, but read them in a truly historical spirit, prepared for many difficulties, undiscouraged by many contradictions, which, so far from disproving the authenticity, become to the historian of ancient language and ancient thought the strongest confirmatory evidence of the age, the genuineness, and the real truth of ancient sacred books. Let us but treat our own sacred books with neither more nor less mercy than the sacred books of any other nations, and they will soon regain that position and influence which they once possessed, but which the artificial and unhistorical theories of the last three centuries have well-nigh destroyed. *Science of Religion.*

By the students of the science of religion the Old Testament can only be looked upon as a strictly historical book, by the side of other historical books. It can claim no privilege before the tribunal of history; nay, to claim such a privilege would be to really deprive it of the high position which it justly holds among the most valuable monuments of the distant past. But the authorship of the single books which form the Old Testament, and more particularly the dates at which they were reduced to writing, form the subject of keen controversy, not among critics hostile to religion, but among theologians who treat these questions in the most independent, but at the same time, the most candid and judicial, spirit. By this treatment many difficulties, which in former times disturbed the minds of thoughtful theologians, have been removed, and the Old Testament has resumed its rightful place among the most valuable monuments of antiquity. . . . But this was possible on one condition only, namely, that the Old Testament should be treated simply as an historical book, willing to submit to all the

tests of historical criticism to which other historical
books have submitted.   *Gifford Lectures, II.*

What the student of the history of the continuous
growth of religion looks for in vain in the books
of the Old Testament, are the successive stages
in the development of religious concepts. He
does not know which books he may consider as
more ancient or more modern than other books.
He asks in vain how much of the religious ideas
reflected in certain of these books may be due
to ancient tradition, how much to the mind of the
latest writer.   In Exodus iii., God is revealed to
Moses, not only as the supreme, but as the only
God.   But we are now told by competent scholars
that Exodus could not have been written down till
probably a thousand years after Moses.   How
then can we rely on it as an accurate picture of the
thoughts of Moses and his contemporaries?   It
has been said with great truth that "it is almost
impossible to believe that a people who had
been emancipated from superstition at the time
of the Exodus, and who had been all along taught
to conceive God as the one universal Spirit,
existing only in truth and righteousness, should be
found at the time of Josiah, nearly 900 years later,
steeped in every superstition."   Still if the writings

of the Old Testament * were contemporaneous
with the events they relate, this retrogressive
movement would have to be admitted. Most of
these difficulties are removed, or considerably
lessened, if we accept the results of modern Hebrew
scholarship, and remember that though the Old
Testament may contain very ancient traditions,
they probably were not reduced to writing till the
middle of the fifth century B. C., and may have
been modified by and mixed up with ideas belonging to the time of Ezra.   *Ibid.*

May we, or may we not, interpret, as students of
language, and particularly as students of Oriental
languages, the language of the Old Testament as
a primitive and as an Oriental language ? May
we, or may we not, as true believers, see through
the veil which human language always throws
over the most sacred mysteries of the soul, and
instead of dragging the sublimity of Abraham's
trial and Abraham's faith down to the level of a
merely preternatural event, recognise in it the

* The reader is reminded that these lectures were published in 1891, before
English theologians had reached any generally received results in the study of
the dates of the various parts of the Old Testament. It would be more cor-
rect now to substitute the " Pentateuch " for the " Old Testament." For a
statement of the modern views of the several periods to which the different
books may be assigned, see Canon Driver's " Introduction to the Literature
of the Old Testament."

real trial of a human soul, the real faith of the friend of God, a faith without stormwinds, without earthquakes and fires, a faith in the still small voice of God ? *MS.*

Is it really necessary to say again and again what the Buddhists have said so often and well, that the act of creation is perfectly inconceivable to any human understanding, and that, if we speak of it at all, we can only do so anthropomorphically, or mythologically ? *MS.*

CHILDREN

ALL seems to bright and perfect, and quite a new life seems to open before me, in that beloved little child. She helps me to look forward to such a far distance and opens quite a new view of one's own purpose and duties on earth. It is something new to live for, to train a human soul intrusted to us, and to fit her for her true home beyond this life.   *Life.*

I doubt whether it is possible to take too high a view of life where the education of children is concerned. It is the one great work intrusted to us, it forms the true religion of life. ? Nothing is small or unimportant in forming the next generation, which is to carry on the work where we have to leave it unfinished. No single soul can be spared—every one is important, every one may be the cause of infinite good, or of infinite mischief, for ever hereafter.   *MS.*

CHRIST. THE LOGOS

An explanation of *Logos* in Greek philosophy is much simpler than is commonly supposed. It is only needful not to forget that for the Greeks thought and word were inseparable, and that the same term, namely, *Logos*, expressed both, though they distinguished the inner from the outer *Logos*. It is one of the most remarkable aberrations of the human mind to imagine that there could be a word without thought, or a thought without word. The two are inseparable; one cannot exist or be even conceived without the other.

Silesian Horseherd.

In nearly all religions God remains far from man. I say, in nearly all religions: for in Brahmanism the unity, not the union, of the human soul with Brahma is recognised as the highest aim. This unity with Deity together with phenomenal difference, Jesus expressed in part through the *Logos*, in part through the Son. There is nothing so closely allied as thought and word, Father and Son. They can be distinguished but never separated, for they exist only through each other.

15

In this manner the Greek philosophers considered all creation as the thought or the word of God, and the thought "man" became naturally the highest *Logos*, realised in millions of men, and raised to the highest perfection in Jesus. As the thought exists only through the word, and the word only through the thought, so also the Father exists only through the Son, and the Son through the Father, and in this sense Jesus feels and declares Himself the Son of God, and all men who believe in Him His brethren. This revelation or inspiration came to mankind through Jesus. No one knew the Father except the Son, Who is in the bosom of the Father, and those to whom the Son willeth to reveal Him. This is the Christian Revelation in the true sense of the word.   *Ibid.*

Small as may be the emphasis that we now lay on the *Logos* doctrine, in that period (i. e. of the Fourth Gospel) it was the centre, the vital germ, of the whole Christian teaching. If we read any of the writings of Athanasius, or of any of the older Church Fathers, we shall be surprised to see how all of them begin with the Word (*Logos*) as a fixed point of departure, and then proceed to prove that the Word is the Son of God, and finally that the Son of God is Jesus of

Nazareth.   Religion and philosophy are here
closely related.   *Ibid.*   ·

What is true Christianity if it be not the belief
in the true sonship of man, as the Greek philosophers had rightly surmised, but had never seen
realised on earth ?   Here is the point where the
two great intellectual currents of the Aryan
and Semitic worlds flow together, in that the long-
expected Messiah of the Jews was recognised as
the *Logos*, the true Son of God, and that He
opened or revealed to every man the possibility
to become what he had always been, but had
never before apprehended, the highest thought,
the Word, the *Logos*, the Son of God.   *Ibid.*

Eternal life consists in knowing that men have
their Father and their true being in the only
true God, and that as sons of this same Father,
they are of like nature with God and Christ.
                                               Ibid.

Why should the belief in the Son give everlasting
life ?   Because Jesus has through His own sonship
in God declared to us ours also.   This knowledge
gives us eternal life through the conviction that

we too have something divine and eternal within us, namely, the word of God, the Son whom He hath sent. Jesus Himself, however, is the only begotten Son, the light of the world. He first fulfilled and illumined the divine idea which lies darkly in all men, and made it possible for all men to become actually what they have always been potentially—sons of God.   *Ibid.*

We make the fullest allowance for those who, from reverence for God and for Christ, and from the purest motives, protest against claiming for man the full brotherhood of Christ. But when they say that the difference between Christ and mankind is one of kind, and not of degree, they know not what they do, they nullify the whole of Christ's teaching, and they deny the Incarnation which they pretend to teach.

Gifford Lectures, IV.

The Ammergau play must be very powerful. And I feel sure just now nothing is more wanted than to be powerfully impressed with the truly human character of Christ; it has almost vanished under the extravagant phraseology of hymns and creeds, and yet how much greater is the simple story of His unselfish life than all the superlatives of later Theology. If one knows what it is to lose a human soul whom one has loved—how one forgets all that was human, and only clings to what was eternal in it, one can understand the feelings of Christ's friends and disciples when they saw Him crucified and sacrificed, the innocent for those whom He wished to guide and save.

MS.

Jesus destroyed the barrier between man and God, the veil that hid the Holiest was withdrawn. Man was taught to see, what the prophets had seen dimly, that he was near to God, that God was near to every one of us, that the old Jewish view of a distant Jehovah had arisen from an excess of reverence, had filled the heart of man with fear, but not with love. Jesus did not teach a new doctrine—but He removed an old error, and that error, that slavish fear of God once removed, the human heart would recover the old trust in God—man would return like a lost son to his lost father—he would feel that if he was anything, he could only be what his God had made him, and wished him to be. And if a name was wanted for that intimate relation between God and man, what better name was there than Father and Son?   *MS.*

Those who deprived Jesus of His real humanity in order to exalt Him above all humanity were really undoing His work. Christ came to teach us, not what He was, but what we are. He had seen that man, unless he himself learned to be the child of God, was lost. All his aspirations were vain unless they all sprang from one deep aspiration, love of God. And how can we love what is totally different from ourselves? If there is in us a likeness, however small, of God, then we can love our God, feel ourselves drawn toward Him, have our true being in Him. That is the essence of Christianity, that is what distinguishes the Christian from all other religions. And yet that very kernel and seed of Christianity is constantly disregarded, is even looked upon with distrust. Was not Christ, who died for us, more than we ourselves? it is said. Or again, are we to make ourselves gods? Christ never says that He is different from ourselves; He never taught as a God might teach. His constant teaching is, that we are His brethren, and that we ought to follow His example, to become like Him, because we were meant to be like Him. In that He has come near to God, as near as a son can be to his father, He is what He was meant to be. We are not, and hence the deep difference between Him and us.   *MS.*

Then it is said, Is not Christ God? Yes, He is, but in His own sense, not in the Jewish nor in the Greek sense, nor in the sense which so many Christians attach to that article of their faith. Christ's teaching is that we are God, that there is in us something divine—that we are nothing if we are not that. He also teaches that through our own fault we are now widely separated from God, as a son may be entirely separated and alienated from his father. But God is a perfect and loving Father. He knows that we can be weak, and yet be good, and when His lost sons return to Him He receives them and forgives them as only a father can forgive. Let us bestow all praise and glory on Christ as the best son of God. Let us feel how unworthy we are to be called His brothers, and the children of God, but let us not lose Christ, and lose our Father whom He came to show us, by exalting Jesus beyond the place which He claimed Himself. Christ never calls Himself the Father, He speaks of His Father with love, but always with humility and reverence. All attempts to find in human language a better expression than that of son have failed. Theologians and philosophers have tried in vain to define more accurately the relation of Christ to the Father, of man to God. They have called Christ another person of the Godhead. Is that better than

Christ's own simple human language, "I go to my Father"? *MS.*

Christ has been made so unreal to us. He has been spoken of in such unmeasured terms that it is very difficult to gain Him back, such as He was, without a fear of showing less reverence and love of Him than others. And yet, unreal expressions are always false expressions—nothing is so bad as if we do not fully mean what we say. Of course we know Christ through His friends only, they tell us what He told them—they represent Him as He appeared to them. What fallible judges they often were they do not disguise, and that, no doubt, raises the value of their testimony, but we can only see Him as they saw Him; the fact remains we know very little of Him. Still enough remains to show that Christ was full of love, that He loved not only His friends, but His enemies. Christ's whole life seems to have been one of love, not of coldness. He perceived our common brotherhood, and what it was based on, our common Father beyond this world, in heaven, as He said. *MS.*

CHRISTIANITY

CHRISTIANITY is Christianity by this one fundamental truth, that as God is the father of man, so
truly, and not poetically, or metaphorically only,
man is the son of God, participating in God's
very essence and nature, though separated from
God by self and sin. This oneness of nature between the Divine and the human does not lower
the concept of God by bringing it nearer to the
level of humanity; on the contrary, it raises the old
concept of man and brings it nearer to its true
ideal. The true relation between God and man
had been dimly foreseen by many prophets and
poets, but Christ was the first to proclaim that
relation in clear and simple language. He called
Himself the Son of God, and He was the firstborn
son of God in the fullest sense of that word. But
He never made Himself equal with the Father in
whom He lived and moved and had His being.
He was man in the new and true sense of the word
and in the new and true sense of the word He was
God. To my mind man is nothing if He does not
participate in the Divine.

Chips from a German Workshop.

23

True Christianity lives, not in our belief, but in our love, in our love of God, and in our love of man, founded on our love of God.   *Ibid.*

True Christianity, I mean the religion of Christ, seems to me to become more and more exalted the more we know and the more we appreciate the treasures of truth hidden in the despised religions of the world.   But no one can honestly arrive at that conviction unless he uses honestly the same measure for all religions. *Science of Religion.*

The position which Christianity from the very beginning took up with regard to Judaism served as the first lesson in comparative theology, and directed the attention even of the unlearned to a comparison of two religions, differing in their conception of the Deity, in their estimate of humanity, in their motives of morality, and in their hope of immortality, yet sharing so much in common that there are but few of the psalms and prayers in the Old Testament in which a Christian cannot heartily join even now, and but few rules of morality which he ought not even now to obey.   *Ibid.*

It was exactly because the doctrine of Christ, more than that of the founders of any other religion, offered in the beginning an expression of the highest truths in which Jewish carpenters, Roman publicans and Greek philosophers could join without dishonesty, that it has conquered the best part of the world. It was because attempts were made from very early times to narrow and stiffen the outward expression of our faith, to put narrow dogma in the place of trust and love, that the Christian Church often lost those who might have been its best defenders, and that the religion of Christ has almost ceased to be what, before all things, it was meant to be, a religion of world-wide love and charity.   *Hibbert Lectures.*

The founder of Christianity insisted again and again on the fact that He came to fulfil, and not to destroy; and we know how impossible it would be to understand the true position of Christianity in the history of the world, the true purport of the "fulness of time," unless we always remember that its founder was born and lived and died an Israelite. Many of the parables and sayings of the New Testament have now been traced back, not only to the Old Testament, but to the Talmud also; and we know how difficult it was at first for any but a Jew to understand the true meaning of the new Christian doctrine.

Gifford Lectures, I.

There is no religion in the whole world which in simplicity, in purity of purpose, in charity, and true humanity, comes near to that religion which Christ taught to His disciples. And yet that very religion, we are told, is being attacked on all sides. The principal reason for this omnipresent unbelief is, I believe, the neglect of our foundations, the disregard of our own bookless religion, the almost disdain of Natural Religion. Even Bishops will curl their lips when you speak to them of that natural and universal *religion* which existed before the advent of our historical religions, nay, without which all historical religions would have been as impossible as poetry is without language. Natural religion may exist and does exist without revealed religion. Revealed religion without natural religion is an utter impossibility. *Ibid.*

There can be no doubt that free inquiry has swept away, and will sweep away, many things which have been highly valued, nay, which were considered essential by many honest and pious minds.   And yet who will say that true Christianity, Christianity which is known by its fruits, is less vigorous now than it has ever been before? There have been discussions in the Christian Church from the time of the Apostles to our own times.   We have passed through them ourselves, we are passing through them now.

Gifford Lectures, II.

When we think of the exalted character of Christ's teaching, may we not ask ourselves once more, What would He have said if He had seen the fabulous stories of His birth and childhood, or if He had thought that His Divine character would ever be made to depend on the historical truth of the *Evangelia Infantiae?*   *Ibid.*

Much of the mere outworks of Christianity cannot hold the ground on which they have been   planted, they have to be given up by force   at   last, when they ought to have been given up long before; and when given up at last, they often tear away with them part of the strength of that faith of which they had previously been not only the buttress outside, but a part of the living framework.

Gifford Lectures, III.

What we call Christianity embraces several fundamental doctrines, but the most important of them all is the recognition of the Divine in man, or, as we call it, the belief in the Divinity of the Son. The belief in God, let us say in God the Father, or the Creator and Ruler of the world, had been elaborated by the Jews, and most of the civilised and uncivilised nations of the world had arrived at it. But when the Founder of Christianity called God His Father, and not only His Father, but the Father of all mankind, He did no longer speak the language of either Jews or Greeks. To the Jews, to claim Divine sonship for man, would have been blasphemy. To the Greeks, Divine sonship would have meant no more than a miraculous, a mythological event. Christ spoke a new language, a language liable, no doubt, to be misunderstood, as all language is; but a language which to those who understood it has imparted a new glory to the face of the whole world. It is well known how this event, the discovery of the Divine in man, which involves a complete change in the spiritual condition of mankind, and marks the great turning point in the history of the world, has been surrounded by a legendary halo, has been obscured, has been changed into mere mythology, so that its real meaning has often been quite forgotten, and has to be discovered again by honest and fearless seeking. Christ had to speak the language of His time, but He gave a new meaning to it, and yet that language has often retained its old discarded meaning in the minds of His earliest, nay sometimes of His latest disciples also. The Divine sonship of which He speaks was not blasphemy as the Jews thought, nor mythology as so many of His own followers imagined, and still imagine. Father and Son, divine and human, were like the old bottles that could hardly hold the new wine; and yet how often have the old broken bottles been preferred to the new wine that was to give new life to the world. *Ibid.*

If we have learnt to look upon Christianity, not as something unreal and unhistorical, but as an integral part of history, of the historical growth of the human race, we can see how all the searchings after the Divine or Infinite in man, were fulfilled in the simple utterances of Christ. His preaching, we are told, brought life and immortality to light. Life, the life of the soul, and immortality, the immortality of the soul, were there and had always been there. But they were brought to light, man was made fully conscious of them,

man remembered his royal birth, when the word
had been spoken by Christ.   *Ibid.*

We must never forget that it was not the principal object of Christ's teaching to make others
believe that He only was divine, immortal, or the
son of God.   He wished them to believe this for
their own sake, for *their own* regeneration.   "As
many as received Him to them gave He power
to become the sons of God."   It might be thought,
at first, that this recognition of a Divine element
in man must necessarily lower the conception of
the Divine.   And so it does in one sense.   It
brings God nearer to us, it bridges over the abyss
by which the Divine and the human were completely separated in the Jewish, and likewise in
many of the pagan religions.   It rends the veil
of the temple.   This lowering, therefore, is
no   real   lowering   of   the   Divine.   It is an
expanding   of   the   concept   of   the   Divine,
and   at   the   same   time   a   raising   of the
concept of humanity, or, rather, a restoration
of what is called human to its true character,
a regeneration, or a second birth, as it is
called by Christ Himself: "Except a man be
born again, he cannot see the kingdom of God."
                                              Ibid.

There is a constant action and reaction in the growth of religious ideas, and the first action by which the Divine was separated from and placed almost beyond the reach of the human mind was followed by a reaction which tried to reunite the two. This process, though visible in many religions, was most pronounced in Judaism in its transition to Christianity. Nowhere had the invisible God been further removed from the visible world than in the ancient Jewish religion, and nowhere have the two been so closely drawn together again and made one as by that fundamental doctrine of Christianity, the Divine sonship of man.   *Gifford Lectures, IV.*

Christ spoke to men, women and children, not to theologians, and the classification of His sayings should be made, not according to theological technicalities, but according to what makes our own heart beat.   *Life.*

The yearning for union or unity with God, which we see as the highest goal in other religions, finds its fullest recognition in Christianity, if but properly understood, that is, if but treated historically, and it is inseparable from our belief in man's full brotherhood with Christ. However imperfect the forms may be in which that human yearning for God has found expression in different religions, it has always been the deepest spring of all religions, and the highest summit reached by Natural Religion. The different bridges that have been thrown across the gulf that seems to separate earth from heaven and man from God may be more or less crude and faulty, yet we may trust that many a faithful soul has been carried across by them to a better home. It is quite true that to speak of a bridge between man and God, even if that bridge is called the Self, is but a metaphor. But how can we speak of these things except in metaphors? To return to God is a metaphor, to stand before the throne of God is a metaphor, to be in Paradise with Christ is a metaphor.　*Gifford Lectures, IV.*

The Christian religion should challenge rather than deprecate comparison. If we find certain doctrines which we thought the exclusive property of Christianity in other religions also, does Christianity lose thereby, or is the truth of these doctrines impaired by being recognised by other teachers also?　*Ibid.*

Love—superseding faith—seems to be the keynote of all Christianity. But the world is still far from true Christianity, and whoever is honest toward himself knows how far away he himself is from the ideal he wishes to reach. One can hardly imagine what this world would be if we were really what we profess to be, followers of Christ. The first thing we have to learn is that we are not what we profess to be. When we have learnt that, we shall at all events be more forbearing, forgiving, and loving toward others. We shall believe in them, give them credit for good intentions, with which, I hope, not hell, but heaven, is paved.   *Life.*

Our religion is certainly better and purer than others, but in the essential points all religions have something in common. They all start with the belief that there is something beyond, and they are all attempts to reach out to it.   *Ibid.*

How little was taught by Christ, and yet that is enough, and every addition is of evil. Love God, love men—that is the whole law and the prophets—not the Creeds and the Catechism and the Articles and the endless theological discussions.

We want no more, and those who try to fulfil that simple law know best how difficult it is, and how our whole life and our whole power are hardly sufficient to fulfil that short law. *MS.*

Christ's teaching is plainly that as He is the Son of God so we are His brothers. His conception of man is a new one, and as that is new, so must His conception of God be new. He lifts up humanity, and brings deity near to humanity, and He expresses their inseparable nature and their separate existences by the best simile which the world supplies, that of Father and Son. He claims no more for Himself than He claims for us. His only excellence is that which is due to Himself—His having been the first to find the Father, and become again His Son, and His having remained in life and death more one with the Father than any one of those who professed to believe in Him, and to follow His example.

MS.

If Jesus was not God, was He, they ask, a mere man? A *mere* man? Is there anything among the works of God, anything next to God, more wonderful, more awful, more holy than man? Much rather should we ask, Was then Jesus a

mere God? Look at the miserable conceptions
which man made to himself as long as he spoke
of gods beside God? It could not be otherwise.
God is one, and he who admits other gods beside
or without Him degrades, nay, denies and destroys
the One God. *A* God is less than man. True
Christianity does not degrade the Godhead, it
exalts manhood, by bringing it back near to God,
as near as it is possible for human thought to
approach the ineffable and inconceivable Majesty
of the true God.   *MS.*

If I ventured to speak of God's purpose at all,
I should say that it is not God's purpose to win
only the spiritually gifted, the humble, the tender
hearted, the souls that are discontented with
their own shortcomings, the souls that find happiness in self-sacrifice—those are His already—but
to win the intellectually gifted, the wise, the cultivated, the clever, or better still, to win them both.
It would be an evil day for Christianity if it could
no longer win the intellectually gifted, the wise,
the cultivated, the clever, and it seems to me the
duty of all who really believe in Christ to show
that Christianity, if truly understood, can win the
highest as well as the humblest intellects.

Gifford Lectures, III.

DEATH

TRUST in God! What He does is well done. What we are, we are through Him; what we suffer, we suffer through His will. We cannot conceive His wisdom, we cannot fathom His Love, but we can trust with a trust stronger than all other trusts that He will not forsake us, when we cling to Him, and call on Him, as His Son, Jesus Christ, has taught us to call on Him, "Our Father." Though this earthly form of ours must perish, all that was good, and pure, and unselfish in us will live. Death has no power over what is of God within us. Death changes and purifies and perfects us; Death brings us nearer to God, where we shall meet again those that are God's, and love them with that godly love which can never perish.   *Life.*

Would that loving Father begin such a work in us, as is now going on, and then destroy it, leave it unfinished? No, what is will be; what really is in us will always be; we shall be because we are. Many things which are now will change, but what we really are we shall always be; and if love forms really part of our very life, that love, changed it may be, purified, sanctified, will be with us, and remain with us through that greatest change which we call death. The pangs of death will be the same for all that, just as the pangs of childbirth seem ordained by God in order to moderate the exceeding joy that a child is born into the world. And as the pain is forgotten when the child is born, so it will be after death—the joy will be commensurate to the sorrow. The sorrow is but the effort necessary to raise ourselves to that new and higher state of being, and without that supreme effort or agony, the new life that waits for us is beyond our horizon, beyond our conception. It is childish to try to anticipate, we cannot know anything about it; we are meant to be ignorant; even the "Divina Commedia" of a great poet and thinker is but child's play, and nothing else. . . . No illusions, no anticipations, only that certainty, that quiet rest in God, that submissive expectation of the soul, which knows that all is good, all comes from God, all tends to God.   *MS.*

As one gets older, death seems hardly to make so wide a gap—a few years more or less, that is all—meantime we know in whose hands we all are, that life is very beautiful, but death has its beauty too. *Life.*

We accustom ourselves so easily to life as a second nature, and in spite of the graves around us, death remains something unnatural, hard and terrifying. That should not be. An early death is terrifying, but as we grow older our thoughts should accustom themselves to passing away at the end of a long life's journey. All is so beautiful, so good, so wisely ordered, that even death can be nothing hard, nothing disturbing; it all belongs to a great plan, which we do not understand, but of which we know that it is wiser than all wisdom, better than all good, that it cannot be otherwise, cannot be better. In faith we can live and we can die—can even see those go before us who came before us, and whom we must follow. All is not according to our will, to our wisdom, but according to a heavenly Will, and those who have once found each other through God's hand will, clinging to His hand, find each other again. *Ibid.*

If we are called away sooner or later we ought to part cheerfully, knowing that this earth could give no more than has been ours, and looking forward to our new home, as to a more perfect state where all that was good and true and unselfish in us will live and expand, and all that was bad and mean will be purified and cast off. So let us work here as long as it is day, but without fearing the night that will lead us to a new and brighter dawn of life. *MS.*

Annihilation . . . is a word without any conceivable meaning. We are—that is enough. What we are does not depend on us; what we shall be neither. We may conceive the idea of change in form, but not of cessation or destruction of substance. People mean frequently by annihilation the loss of conscious personality, as distinct from material annihilation. What I feel about it is shortly this. If there is anything real and substantial in our conscious personality, then whatever there is real and substantial in it cannot cease to exist. If on the contrary we mean by conscious personality something that is the result of accidental circumstances, then, no doubt, we must face the idea of such a personality ceasing to be what it now is. I believe, however, that the true source and essence of our personality lies in what is the most real of all real things, and in so far as it is true, it cannot be destroyed. There is a distinction between conscious personality and personal consciousness. A child has personal consciousness, a man who is this or that, a Napoleon, a Talleyrand, has conscious personality. Much of that conscious personality is merely temporary, and passes away; but the personal consciousness remains. *Life.*

One look up to heaven, and all this dust of the high road of life vanishes. Yes! one look up to heaven and that dark shadow of death vanishes. We have made the darkness of that shadow ourselves, and our thoughts about death are very ungodly. God has willed it so; there is to be a change, and a change of such magnitude that even if angels were to come down and tell us all about it, we could not understand it, as little as the newborn child would understand what human language could tell about the present life. Think what the birth of a child, of a human soul, is; and when you have felt the utter impossibility of fathoming that mystery, then turn your thoughts upon death, and see in it a new birth equally unfathomable, but only the continuation of that joyful mystery which we call a birth. It is all God's work, and where is there a flaw in that wonder of all wonders,

God's ever-working work ?   If people talk of the
miseries of life are they not all man's work ?

Ibid.

Great happiness makes one feel so often that it
cannot last, and that we will have some day to
give up all to which one's heart clings so. A few
years sooner or later, but the time will come, and
come quicker than one expects. Therefore I
believe it is right to accustom oneself to the
thought that we can none of us escape death, and
that all our happiness here is only lent us. But
at the same time we can thankfully enjoy all that
God gives us . . . and there is still so much
left us, so much to be happy and thankful for, and
yet here too the thought always rushes across one's
brightest hours: it cannot last, it is only for a few
years and then it must be given up. Let us work
as long as it is day, let us try to do our duty, and
be very thankful for God's blessings which have
been showered upon us so richly—but let us learn
also always to look beyond, and learn to be ready
to give up everything—and yet say, Thy Will be
done.   *MS.*

It is the most painful work I know looking
through the papers and other things belonging to

one who is no more with us. How different everything looks to what it did before. There is one
beautiful feature about death, it carries off all the
small faults of the soul we loved, it makes us see
the true littleness of little things, it takes away all
the shadows, and only leaves the light. That is
how it ought to be, and if in judging of a person
we could only bring ourselves to think how we
should judge of them if we saw them on the bed
of death, how different life would be! We always
judge in self-defence, and that makes our judgments so harsh. When they are gone how readily
we forget and forgive everything, how truly we
love all that was loveable in them, how we blame
ourselves for our own littleness in minding this
and that, and not simply and truly loving all
that was good and bright and noble. How different life might be if we could all bring ourselves to
be what we really are, good and loving, and could
blow away the dust that somehow or other will
fall on all of us. It is never too late to begin
again.   *Life.*

' The death of those we love is the last lesson we
receive in life—the rest we must learn for ourselves.
To me, the older I grow, and the nearer I feel that
to me the end must be, the more perfect and

beautiful all seems to be; one feels surrounded and
supported everywhere by power, wisdom, and
love, content to trust and wait, incapable of mur-
muring, very helpless, very weak, yet strong in
that very helplessness, because it teaches us to
trust in something not ourselves. Yet parting
with those we love is hard—only I fear there is
nothing else that would have kept our eyes open
to what is beyond this life.   *MS.*

It is strange how little we all think of death as
the condition of all the happiness we enjoy now.
If we could but learn to value each hour of life,
to enjoy it fully, to use it fully, never to spoil a
minute by selfishness, then death would never
come too soon; it is the wasted hours which are
like death in life, and which make life really so
short.   It is not too late to learn to try to be more
humble, more forbearing, more courteous, or,
what is at the root of all, more loving.   *Life.*

The great world for which we live seems to me
as good as the little world in which we live, and I
have never known why faith should fail, when
everything, even pain and sorrow, is so wonderfully good and beautiful.   All that we say to con-

sole ourselves on the death of those we loved, and who loved us, is hollow and false; the only true thing is rest and silence. We cannot understand, and therefore we must and can trust. There can be no mistake, no gap, in the world poem to which we belong; and I believe that those stars which without their own contrivance have met will meet again. How, where, when? God knows this, and that is enough.   *MS*.

God has taught us that death is not so terrible as it appears to most men—it is but a separation for a few short days, and then, too, eternity awaits us.   *Life*.

We live here in a narrow dwelling house, which presses us in on all sides, and yet we fancy it is the whole universe. But when the door opens and a loved one passes out, never to return, we too step to the door and look out into the distance, and realise then how small and empty the dwelling is, and how a larger, more beautiful world waits for us without. How it is in that larger world, who can say? But if we were so happy in the narrow dwelling, how far more happy shall we be out there! Be not afraid. See how beautifully all is ordered, look up to the widespread firmament, and think how small it is in comparison with God's almighty power. He who regulates the courses of the stars will regulate the fate of the souls of men, and those souls who have once met, shall they not meet again like the stars ?   *MS.*

Those who are absent are often nearer to us than those who are present.   *MS.*

We reckon too little with death, and then when it comes it overwhelms us. We know all the time that our friends must go, and that we must go, but we shut our eyes, and enjoy their love and friendship as if life could never end. We should say good-bye to each other every evening—perhaps the last good-bye would find us then less unprepared.   *MS.*

There is something so natural in death. We come and we go, there is no break.   *Life.*

What is more natural in life than death ? and having lived this long life, so full of light, having been led so kindly by a Fatherly hand through all storms and struggles, why should I be afraid when I have to make the last step ?   *Ibid.*

THE DEITY

WE clearly see that the possibility of intercourse between man and God, and a revelation of God to man, depends chiefly or exclusively on the conception which man has previously formed of God and man. In all theological researches we must carefully bear in mind that the idea of God is *our* idea, which we have formed in part through tradition, and in part by our own thinking. God is and remains *our* God. We can have a knowledge of Him only through our inner consciousness, not through our senses. *Silesian Horseherd.*

Our duties toward God and man, our love for God and for man, are as nothing without the firm foundation which is formed only by our faith in God, as the Thinker and Ruler of the world, the Father of the Son, who was revealed through Him as the Father of all sons, of all men. *Ibid.*

Though Christianity has given us a purer and truer idea of the Godhead, of the majesty of His

power, and the holiness of His will, there remains
with many of us the conception of a merely objective Deity. God is still with many of us in the
clouds, so far removed from the earth and so high
above anything human, that in trying to realise
fully the meaning of Christ's teaching we often
shrink from approaching too near to the blinding
effulgence of Jehovah. The idea that we should
stand to Him in the relation of children to their
father seems to some people almost irreverent, and
the thought that God is near us everywhere, the
belief that we are also His offspring, nay, that there
has never been an absolute barrier between
divinity and humanity, has often been branded as
Pantheism. Yet Christianity would not be Christianity without this so-called Pantheism, and it is
only some lingering belief in something like a Jove-
like *Deus Optimus Maximus* that keeps the eyes
of our mind fixed with awe on the God of Nature
without, rather than on the much more awful
God of the soul within.

Chips from a German Workshop.

The idea of God is the result of an unbroken
historical evolution, call it a development, an
unveiling, or a purification, but not of a sudden
revelation. . . . What right have we to find
fault with the manner in which the Divine revealed

itself, first to the eyes, and then to the mind, of man? Is the revelation in nature really so contemptible a thing that we can afford to despise it, or at the utmost treat it as good enough for the heathen world? Our eyes must have grown very dim, our mind very dull, if we can no longer perceive how the heavens declare the glory of God.

Gifford Lectures, II.

A belief in one Supreme God, even if at first it was only a henotheistic, and not yet a monotheistic belief, took possession of the leading spirits of the Jewish race at a very early time. All tradition assigns that belief in One God, the Most High, to Abraham. Abraham, though he did not deny the existence of the gods worshipped by the neighbouring tribes, yet looked upon them as different from, and as decidedly inferior to, his own God. His monotheism was, no doubt, narrow. His God was the friend of Abraham, as Abraham was the friend of God. Yet the concept of God formed by Abraham was a concept that could and did grow. Neither Moses, nor the Prophets, nor Christ Himself, nor even Mohammed, had to introduce a new God. Their God was always called the God of Abraham, even when freed from all that was local and narrow in the faith of that patriarch. *Ibid.*

To some any attempt to trace back the name and concept of Jehovah to the same hidden sources from which other nations derived their first intimation of deity, may seem almost sacrilegious. They forget the difference between the human concept of the Deity and the Deity itself, which is beyond the reach of all human concepts. But the historian reads deeper lessons in the growth of these human concepts, as they spring up everywhere in the minds of men who have been seekers after truth—seeking the Lord if haply they might feel after Him and find Him; and when he can show the slow but healthy growth of the noblest and sublimest thoughts out of small and apparently insignificant beginnings, he rejoices as the labourer rejoices over his golden harvest; nay, he often wonders what is more truly wonderful, the butterfly that soars up to heaven on its silvery wings, or the grub that hides within its mean chrysalis such marvellous possibilities. *Ibid.*

The concept of God arises by necessity in the human mind, and is not, as so many theologians will have it, the result of one special disclosure, granted to Jews and Christians only. It seems to me impossible to resist this conviction, where a comparative study of the great religions of the world shows us that the highest attributes which we claim for the Deity are likewise ascribed to it by the Sacred Books of other religions.   *Ibid.*

We can now repeat the words which have been settled for us centuries ago, and which we have learnt by heart in our childhood—I believe in God the Father, Maker of heaven and earth—with the conviction that they express, not only the faith of the apostles, or of œcumenical councils, but that they contain the Confession of Faith of the whole world, expressed in different ways, conveyed in thousands of languages, but always embodying the same fundamental truth. I call it fundamental, because it is founded in the very nature of our mind, our reason and our language, on a simple and ineradicable conviction that where there are acts there must be agents, and in the end, one Prime Agent, whom man may know, not indeed in His own inscrutable essence, yet in His acts, as revealed in Nature.   *Ibid.*

The historical proof of the existence of God, which is supplied to us by the history of the religions of the world, has never been refuted, and cannot be refuted. It forms the foundation of all the other proofs, call them cosmological, ontological, or teleological, or rather it absorbs them all, and makes them superfluous. There are those who declare that they require no proof at all for the existence of a Supreme Being, or if they did, they would find it in revelation, and nowhere else. Suppose they wanted no proof themselves, would they really not care at all to know how the human race, and how they themselves, came in possession of what, I suppose, they value as their most precious inheritance? An appeal to revelation is of no avail in deciding questions of this kind, unless it is first explained what is really meant by revelation. The history of religions teaches us that the same appeal to a special revelation is made, not only by Christianity, but by the defenders of Brahmanism, Zoroastrianism and Mohammedanism, and where is the tribunal to adjudicate on the conflicting appeals of these and other claimants? The followers of every one of these religions declare their belief in the revealed character of their own religion, never in that of any other religion. There is, no doubt, a revelation to which we may appeal in the court of our own conscience, but before the court of universal appeal we require different proofs for the faith that is in us.

Gifford Lectures, III.

Given man, such as he is, and given the world, such as it is, a belief in divine beings, and, at last, in one Divine Being, is not only a universal, but an inevitable fact. . . . If from the standpoint of human reason, no flaw can be pointed out in the intellectual process which led to the admission of something within, behind, or beyond nature, call it the Infinite or any other name you like, it follows that the history of that process is really, at the same time, the best proof of the legitimacy and truth of the conclusions to which it has led. *Ibid.*

There is no predicate in human language worthy of God, all we can say of Him is what the Upanishads said of Him, No, No! What does that mean? It meant that if God is called all-powerful, we have to say No, because whatever we comprehend by powerful is nothing compared with the power of God. If God is called all-wise, we have again to say No, because what we call wisdom cannot approach the wisdom of God. If God is called holy, again we have to say No, for what can our conception of holiness be, compared with the holiness of God? This is what the thinkers of the Upanishads meant when they said that all we can say of God is No, No. *Ibid.*

If people would only define what they mean by knowing, they would shrink from the very idea that God can ever be known by us in the same sense in which everything else is known, or that with regard to Him we could ever be anything but Agnostics. All human knowledge begins with the senses, and goes on from sensations to percepts, from percepts to concepts and names. And yet the same people who insist that they know God, will declare in the same breath that no one can see God and live. Let us only define the meaning of knowing, and keep the different senses in which this word has been used carefully apart, and I doubt whether anyone would venture to say that, in the true sense of the word, he is not an Agnostic as regards the true nature of God. This silence before a nameless Being does not exclude a true belief in God, nor devotion, nor love of a Being beyond our senses, beyond our understanding, beyond our reason, and therefore beyond all names.   *Ibid.*

Every one of the names given to this infinite Being by finite beings marks a stage in the evolution of religious truth. If once we try to understand these names, we shall find that they were all well meant, that, for the time being, they were probably the only possible names. The Historical School does not look upon all the names given to divine powers as simply true, or simply false. We look upon all of them as well meant and true for the time being, as steps on the ladder on which the angels of God ascend and descend. There was no harm in the ancient people, when they were thirsting for rain, invoking the sky, and saying, "O dear sky, send us rain!" And when after a time they used more and more general words, when they addressed the powers (of nature) as bright, or rich, or mighty, all these were meant for something else, for something they were seeking for, if haply they might feel after Him and find Him. This is St. Paul's view of the growth of religion. *Ibid.*

When God has once been conceived without "any manner of similitude," He may be meditated on, revered, and adored, but that fervent passion of the human breast, that love with all our heart, and all our soul, and all our might, seems to become hushed before that solemn presence. We may love our father and mother with all our heart, we may cling to our children with all our soul, we may be devoted to wife, or husband, or friend, with all our might, but to throw all these feelings in their concentrated force and truth on the Deity has been given to very few on earth.   *Ibid.*

If the history of religion has taught us any-thing, it has taught us to distinguish between the names and the thing named. The names may change, and become more and more perfect, and our concepts of the deity may become more perfect also, but the deity itself is not affected by our names. However much the names may differ and change, there remains, as the last result of the study of religion, the everlasting conviction that behind all the names there is something named, that there is an agent behind all acts, that there is an Infinite behind the Finite, that there is a God in Nature; that God is the abiding goal of many names, all well meant and well aimed, and yet all far, far away from the goal which no man can see and live. All names that human language has invented may be imperfect. But the name "I am that I am" will remain for those who think Semitic thought, while to those who speak Aryan languages it will be difficult to invent a better name than the Vedanta Sak-kid-ânanda, He who is, who knows, who is blessed.   *Ibid.*

However much we may cease to speak the language of the faith of our childhood, the faith in a superintending and ever-present Providence grows only stronger the more we see of life, the more we know of ourselves. When that bass-note is right, we may indulge in many variations —we shall never go entirely wrong.   *MS.*

We do not see the hand that takes our dear ones from us, but we know whose hand it is, whose will it is. We have no name for Him, we do not know Him, but we know that whatever name we give, He will understand it. That is the foundation of all religion. Let us give the best name we can find in us, let us know that even that must be a very imperfect name, but let us trust that if we only believe in that name, if we use it, not because it is the fashion, but because we can find no better name, He will understand and forgive. Every name is true, if we are true; every name is false, if we are false. If we are true, our religion is true; if we are false our religion is false. An honest fetish worshipper even is better than a scoffing Pope.
     MS.

In the ordinary sense of knowledge, we cannot have any knowledge of God; our very idea of

God implies that He is beyond our powers of perception and understanding. Then what can we do? Shut our eyes and be silent? That will not satisfy creatures such as we are. We must speak, but all our words apply to things perceptible or intelligible. The old Buddhists used to say, The only thing we can say of God is No, No! He is not this, He is not that. Whatever we can see or understand, He is not that. But again I say that kind of self-denial will not satisfy such creatures as we are. What can we do? We can only give the best we have. Now the best we have or know on earth is Love, therefore we say God is Love or loving. Love is entire self-surrender, we can go no further in our conception of what is best. And yet how poor a name it is in comparison of what we want to name. Our idea of love includes humility, a looking up and worshipping. Can we say that of God's love? Depend upon it, the best we say is but poor endeavour—it is well we should know it—and yet, if it is the best we have and can give, we need not be ashamed. *Life.*

And now that generations after generations have passed away, with their languages—adoring and worshipping the Name of God—preaching

and dying in the Name of God—thinking and
meditating on the Name of God—there the old
word stands still, breathing to us the pure air of
the dawn of humanity, carrying with it all the
thoughts and sighs, the doubts and tears, of our
bygone brethren, and still rising up to heaven
with the same sound from the basilicas of Rome
and the temples of Benares, as if embracing by
its simple spell millions and millions of hearts in
their longing desire to give utterance to the unutterable, to express the inexpressible.   *Ibid.*

THE DIVINE

IT was, after all, the Jew who, in the great history of the world, was destined to solve the riddle of the Divine in man. It was the soil of Jewish thought that in the end gave birth to the true conception of the relation between the Divine in nature and the Divine in man.

Gifford Lectures, III.

When the Divine in the outward world has once been fully recognised, there can be nothing more or less divine, nothing more or less miraculous, either in nature or in history. Those who assign a divine and miraculous character to certain consecrated events only in the history of the world, are in great danger of desecrating thereby the whole drama of history, and of making it, not only profane, but godless. It is easy to call this a pantheistic view of the world. It is pantheistic, in the best sense of the word, so much so that any other view would soon become atheistic. Even the Greeks suspected the omnipresence of the Divine, when, as early as the time of Thales, they

declared that *all* is full of the gods. The choice
here lies really between Pantheism and Atheism.
If anything, the greatest or the smallest, can ever
happen without the will of God, then God is no
longer God. To distinguish between a direct and
indirect influence of the Divine, to admit a general
and a special providence, is like a relapse into
Polytheism, a belief in one and many gods.

Ibid.

Human nature is divine nature modified. It
can be nothing else. Christ, in shaking off all
that is not Divine in man, let us call it by one
general name, all that is selfish, resumed His own
divinity.   *MS.*

God comes to us in the likeness of man—there
is no other likeness for God. And that likeness
is not forbidden; Christ has taught us to see and
love God in man. We cannot go further. If
we attempt to conceive anything more than
human, our mind breaks down. But we can conceive and perceive the Divine in man, and most
in those who are risen from the earth. While
we live our love is human, and mixed with earthly
things. We love and do not love—we even hate,
or imagine we do. But we do not really hate

any man, we only hate something that surrounds and hides man. What is behind, the true nature of man, we always love. Death purifies man, it takes away the earthly crust, and we can love those who are dead far better than those who are still living: that is the truth. We do not deceive ourselves, we do not use vain words. Love is really purer, stronger and more unselfish, when it embraces those who are risen. That is why the Apostles loved Christ so much better when He was no longer with them. While He lived, Peter could deny Him—when He had returned to the Father, Peter was willing to die for Him. All that is so true, only one must have gone through it, felt it oneself in order to understand it. If one knows the love one feels for the blessed, one wants no temporary resurrection to account for the re-kindled love of the Apostles. They believed that Christ had truly risen, that death had no power over Him, that He was with the Father. Was not that more, far more, than a return to this fleeting life for a few hours, or days, or weeks, or than an ascent through the clouds to the blue sky? Ah! how the great truths have been exchanged for small fancies, the *mira* for the *miracula.*

MS.

DOUBTS

There is an atheism which is unto death, there is another atheism which is the life blood of all true faith. It is the power of giving up what, in our best, our most honest, moments, we know to be no longer true; it is the readiness to replace the less perfect, however dear, however sacred it may have been to us, by the more perfect, however much it may be detested, as yet, by the world. It is the true self-surrender, the true self-sacrifice, the truest trust in truth, the truest faith. Without that atheism religion would long ago have become a petrified hypocrisy; without that atheism no new religion, no reform, no reformation, no resuscitation would ever have been possible; without that atheism no new life is possible for any one of us.   *Hibbert Lectures.*

There is certainly no happier life than a life of simple faith; of literal acceptance, of rosy dreams. We must all grant that, if it were possible, nothing would be more perfect. I gladly acknowledge that some of the happiest, and also some of the

63

best men and women I have known, were those who would have shrunk with horror from questioning a single letter of the Bible, or doubting that a serpent actually spoke to Eve, and an ass to Balaam. But can we prevent the light of the sun and the noises of the street from waking the happy child from his heavenly dreams? Nay, is it not our duty to wake the child, when the time has come that he must be up and doing, and take his share in the toils of the day? And is it not well for those who for the first time open their eyes and look around, that they should see by their side some who have woke before them, who understand their inquiring looks, and can answer their timid questions and tell them in the simple-hearted language of the old poet:

"There lives more faith in honest doubt,
    Believe me, than in half the creeds."

Gifford Lectures, III.

How many men in all countries and all ages have been called atheists, not because they denied that there existed anything beyond the visible and the finite, or because they declared that the world, such as it was, could be explained without a cause, without a purpose, without a God, but often because they differed only from the traditional conception of the Deity prevalent at the time, and were yearning after a higher conception of God than what they had learnt in their childhood.

Ibid.

There are moments in our life when those who seek most earnestly after God think they are forsaken of God; when they hardly venture to ask themselves, Do I then believe in God, or do I not? Let them not despair, and let us not judge harshly of them; their despair may be better than many creeds. . . . Honest doubt is the deepest spring of honest faith; only he who has lost can find.

Ibid.

If we have once claimed the freedom of the spirit which St. Paul claimed: to prove all things and hold fast that which is good: we cannot turn back, we cannot say that no one shall prove our own religion, no one shall prove other religions and compare them with our own. We have to choose once for all between freedom and slavery of judgment, and though I do not wish to argue with those who prefer slavery, yet one may remind them that even they, in deliberately choosing slavery, follow their own private judgment, quite as much as others do in choosing freedom.

Gifford Lectures, III.

Our own self interest surely would seem to suggest as severe a trial of our own religion as of other religions, nay, even a more severe trial. Our religion has sometimes been compared to a good ship that is to carry us through the waves and tempests of this life to a safe haven. Would it not be wise, therefore, to have it tested, and submitted to the severest trials, before we intrust ourselves and those dear to us to such a vessel. And remember, all men, except those who take part in the foundation of a new religion, or have been converted from an old to a new faith, have to accept their religious belief on trust, long before they are able to judge for themselves. And while in all other matters an independent judgment in riper years is encouraged, every kind of influence is used to discourage a free examination of religious dogmas, once engrafted on our intellect in its tenderest stage. We condemn an examination of our own religion, even though it arises from an honest desire to see with our own eyes the truth which we mean to hold fast; and yet we do not hesitate to send missionaries into all the world, asking the faithful to re-examine their own time-honoured religions. We attack their most sacred convictions, we wound their tenderest feelings, we undermine the belief in which they have been brought up, and we break up the peace and happiness of their homes. Yet, if some learned Jew, or subtle Brahman, or outspoken Zulu, asks us to re-examine the date and authorship of the Old or New Testament, or challenges us to produce the evidence on which we also are quite ready to accept certain miracles, we are offended, forgetting that with regard to these questions we can claim no privilege, no immunity.

Ibid.

If we can respect a childlike and even a childish faith, we ought likewise to learn to respect even a philosophical atheism which often contains the hidden seeds of the best and truest faith. We ought never to call a man an atheist, and say that he does not believe in God, till we know what kind of God it is he has been brought up to believe in, and what kind of God it is that he rejects, it may be, from the best and highest motives. We ought never to forget that Socrates was called an atheist, that the early Christians were all called atheists, that some of the best and greatest men this world has ever known have been branded by that name.

Ibid.

I have heard and read the worst that can be said against our religion—I mean the true original teaching of Christ—and I feel that I am ready in mind, if not in body, to lay down my life for the truth of His teaching. All our difficulties arise from the doctrines of men, not from His doctrine. There is no outward evidence of the truth of His doctrine, but the Spirit of God that is within us testifieth to its truth.   If it does not, we are not yet disciples of Christ, but we may be hereafter.

Life.

Be certain of this, that to repress a doubt is to repress the spirit of truth; a doubt well spoken out is generally a doubt solved.   But all this requires great seriousness of mind—it must assume an importance greater than anything else in life, and then we can fight our way through it.   God is with us in our struggles.   *Ibid.*

EVOLUTION OF RELIGION

EVOLUTION is really the same as history, if we take it in its objective sense. Subjectively, history meant originally inquiry, or a desire to know; it then came to mean knowledge, obtained by inquiry; and lastly, in a purely objective sense, the objects of such knowledge.   *Gifford Lectures, I.*

We may discover in all the errors of mythology, and in what we call the false or pagan religions of this world, a progress toward truth, a yearning after something more than finite, a growing recognition of the Infinite, throwing off some of its veils before our eyes, and from century to century revealing itself to us more and more in its own purity and holiness.   And thus the two concepts, that of evolution and that of revelation, which seem at first so different, become one in the end.   If there is a purpose running through the ages, if nature is not blind, if there are agents, recognised at last as the agents of one Will, behind the whole phenomenal world, then the evolution of man's belief in that Supreme Will is itself the truest revelation of that

Supreme Will, and must remain the adamantine foundation on which all religion rests, whether we call it natural or supernatural.

Gifford Lectures, II.

The same changes in the idea of God, which we see in the different books of the Bible, take place in the different chapters of our own life. The child cannot but represent God to himself as a venerable man, walking about, warning and reproving the creatures He has made. The child has no higher conception as yet, which it could apply to God; if it heard of a higher one it could not grasp it. But as the child grows and gathers in higher conceptions, the lower must give way to the higher. As long as the evidence of the senses is the only evidence which a child knows, he demands a visible God. When he learns that the human senses are different modes of apprehension, that according to their very nature they can never apprehend except what is limited, then the mind involuntarily surrenders the visible God, it believes in God as a Spirit. And so the growth of each man, and the growth of the whole human race, goes on, and will go on, and I cannot see how, if the world goes on as it has hitherto, it can be otherwise but that much of the language of the New Testament also will have to be surrendered.

Changes have lately taken place with the word *person!* Many things which were formerly comprehended under personality, have been discovered to be mere accessories, and above the more material conception of personality, of individuality, or of the I, a higher one is rising, that of the *Self.* The I, the personality, is made up of many things which are purely temporal—which are dear to us on earth, but which will pass away, while the Self will abide for ever. Need we wonder therefore that just those who wish to transfer only their highest to the Godhead begin to shrink from speaking of a personal God? or insist on defining the word personal so that it should exclude all that is incompatible with a perfect, unlimited, unchanging Being? What led to such expressions as, God is Love, but a feeling of reverence, which shrank from speaking of God as loving as we love? This process will go on as long as the thoughts and words of mankind grow and change. Let us learn only from the Bible that those who spoke of God as walking about in Paradise, spoke as children, did the best they could, gave all they had, and who shall say that their two mites were in the sight of God less precious than all our creeds and philosophies? They too will change, they too will be looked upon by future generations as the language of children. But He to whom our thoughts and prayers are addressed will interpret all languages and dialects. Before Him the wisdom of the man will not sound much wiser than the trustful ignorance of the child.   *MS.*

FAITH

NEXT to our faith in God there is nothing so essential to the healthy growth of our whole being as an unshaken faith in man.

Chips from a German Workshop.

Let us trust in Him to whom alone we owe all our blessings—if we do not forsake Him, He will never forsake us—we cannot fathom His love, but we can trust. *MS.*

Separation loses its bitterness when we have faith in each other and in God. Faith in each other keeps us close together in life, and faith in God keeps us together in eternity. *MS.*

Those who remember the happiness of the simple faith of their childhood may well ask why it should ever be disturbed. Knowing the blessedness of that faith we naturally abstain from everything that might disturb it prematurely in the minds of those who are

73

intrusted to us. But, as the child, whether he likes it or not, grows to be a man, so the faith of a child grows into the faith of a man. It is not our doing, it is the work of Him who made us what we are. As all our other ideas grow and change, so does our idea of God. I know there are men and women who, when they perceive the first warnings of that inward growth, become frightened and suppress it with all their might. They shut their eyes and ears to all new light from within and from without. They wish to remain as happy as children, and many of them succeed in remaining as good as children. Who would blame them or disturb them? But those who trust in God and God's work within them, must go forth to the battle. With them it would be cowardice and faithlessness to shrink from the trial. They are not certain that they were meant to be here simply to enjoy the happiness of a child-like faith. They feel they have a talent committed to them which must not be wrapped up in a napkin. But the battle is hard, and all the harder because while they know they are obeying the voice of truth, which is the voice of God, many of those whom they love look upon them as disobeying the voice of God, as disturbers of the peace, as giving offence to those little ones. *MS.*

There is a difference between the childlike faith of a man (all real faith must be childlike) and the childlike faith of a child. The one is Paradise not yet lost, the other Paradise lost but regained. The one is right for the child, the other is right for the man. It is the will of God that it should be so —but it is also the will of God that we should all bear with each other, and join, each in his own voice, in the great hymn of praise. *MS.*

Faith is that organ of knowledge by which we apprehend the Infinite, namely, whatever transcends the ken of our senses and the grasp of our reason. The Infinite is hidden from the senses, it is denied by Reason, but it is perceived by Faith; and it is perceived, if once perceived, as underlying both the experience of the senses and the combinations of reason. *Science of Language.*

THE FATHERHOOD OF GOD

WHEREVER our Father leads us there is our Fatherland. *Life.*

Man must discover that God is his Father before he can become a son of God. To know is here to be, to be to know. No mere miracle will make man the son of God. That sonship can be gained through knowledge only, "through man knowing God, or rather being known of God," and till it is so gained, it does not exist, even though it be a fact. If we apply this to the words in which Christ speaks of Himself as the Son of God, we shall see that to Him it is no miracle, it is no mystery, it is no question of supernatural contrivance; it is simply clear knowledge, and it was this self-knowledge which made Christ what He was, it was this which constituted His true, His eternal divinity. *Gifford Lectures, III.*

FUTURE LIFE

ONE wonders indeed how kindred souls become separated, and one feels startled and repelled at the thought that, such as they were on earth, they can never meet again.   And yet there is continuity in the world, there is no flaw, no break anywhere, and what has been will surely be again, though how it will be we cannot know, and if only we trust in the Wisdom that pervades and overshadows the whole Universe, we need not know.

Auld Lang Syne.

Even if we resign ourselves to the thought that the likenesses and likelihoods which we project upon the unseen and unknown, nay, that the hope of our meeting again as we once met on earth, need not be fulfilled exactly as we shape them to ourselves, where is the argument to make us believe that the real fulfilment can be less perfect than what even a weak human heart devises and desires ? This trust that whatever is will be best, is what is meant by faith, true, because inevitable, faith. We see traces of it in many places and many religions, but I doubt whether anywhere that faith is more simply and more powerfully expressed than in the Old and New Testaments: "For since the beginning of the world men have not heard, nor perceived by the ear, neither hath the eye seen, Oh God beside Thee, what He hath prepared for him that waiteth for Him" (Isaiah, lxiv. 4). "As it is written, Eye hath not seen nor ear heard, neither have entered into the heart of man, the things which God hath prepared for them that love Him" (I. Cor. ii., 9).

Hibbert Lectures.

The highest which man can comprehend is man. One step only he may go beyond, and say that what is beyond may be different, but it cannot be less perfect than the present; the future cannot be worse than the past. . . . That much-decried philosophy of evolution, if it teaches us anything, teaches us a firm belief in a better future, and in a higher perfection which man is destined to reach. *Ibid.*

In our longings for the departed we often think of them as young or old; we think of them as man or woman, as father or mother, as husband or wife. Even nationality and language are supposed to remain after death, and we often hear expressions, "Oh! if the souls are without all this, without age, and sex, and national character, without even their native language, what will they be to us?" The answer is, they will really be the same to us they were in this life. Unless we can bring ourselves to believe that a soul has a beginning, and that our soul sprang into being at the time of our birth, the soul within us must have existed before. But however convinced we may be of the soul's eternal existence, we shall always remain ignorant as to how it existed. And yet we do not murmur or complain. Our soul on awakening here is not quite a stranger to itself, and the souls who as our parents, our wives, and husbands, our children, and our friends, have greeted us at first as strangers in this life, have become to us as if we had known them forever, and as if we could never lose them again. If it were to be so again in the next life, if there also we should meet at first as strangers till drawn together by the same mysterious love that has drawn us together here, why should we murmur or complain? Thousands of years ago we read of a husband telling his wife, "Verily a wife is not dear that you may love the wife, but that you may love the soul, therefore a wife is dear." What does that mean? It means that true love consists not in loving what is perishable, but in discovering and loving what is eternal in man or woman. In Sanscrit that eternal part is called by many names, but the best seems that used in this passage, Atma. We translate it by Soul, but it is even higher and purer than Soul, it is best translated by the word *Self*. That which constitutes the true Self, the looker on, the witness within us, that which is everywhere in the body and yet nowhere to be touched, that which cannot die or expire, because it never breathed, that is the Infinite in man which philosophers have been groping for, though "he is not far from every one of us." It is the Divine or God-like in man.

Gifford Lectures, III.

The southern Aryans were absorbed in the struggles of thought; their past is the problem of creation, their future the problem of existence, and the present, which ought to be the solution of both, seems never to have attracted their attention or called forth their energies. There never was a nation believing so firmly in another world, and so little concerned about this. Their condition on earth was to them a problem; their real and eternal life a simple fact. Though this is true chiefly before they were brought in contact with foreign conquerors, traces of this character are still visible in the Hindus as described by the companions of Alexander, nay, even in the Hindus of the present day.   The only sphere in which the Indian mind finds itself at liberty to act, to create, and to worship, is the sphere of religion and philosophy, and nowhere have religious and metaphysical ideas struck root so deeply in the mind of a nation as in India.   History supplies no second instance where the inward life of the soul has so completely absorbed all the other faculties of a people.

India.

Our happiness here is but a foretaste of our blessed life hereafter.   We must never forget that. We shall be called away, but we shall meet again.

Life.

We must have patience—and we all cling to life as long as there are those who love us here.   Those who love us there are always ours. Nothing is lost in the world.   How it will be, we know not, but if we have recognised the working of a divine wisdom and love here on earth, we can take comfort, and wait patiently for that which is to come.   *Ibid.*

Truly those who die young are blest.   And shall we find them again such as they left us?

Why not? It is really here on earth that those whom we love change, it is here that they die every day. . . . Where are all those bright joyous faces which we look at when we open our photograph books from year to year? On earth they are lost, but are they not treasured up for another life, where we shall be not only what we are from day to day, never the same to-morrow as we were yesterday, but where we are at once all that we can be—where memory is not different from perception, nor our wills different from our acts? We shall soon know—till then surely we have a right to be what we are, and to cling to our human hopes. The more human they are, the nearer the truth they are likely to be.

Ibid.

I believe in all our hopes we cannot be human enough. Let us be what we are—men, feel as men, sorrow as men, hope as men. It is true our hopes are human, but what are the doubts and difficulties? Are they not human too? Shall we meet again as we left? Why not? We do not know *how* it will be so, but who has a right to say it *cannot* be so? Let us imagine and hope for the best that, as men, we can conceive, and then rest convinced that it will be a thousand times better.

Ibid.

The inward voice never suggested or allowed me the slightest doubt or misgiving about the reality of a future life. If there is continuity in the world everywhere why should there be a wrench and annihilation only with us? It will be as it has been—that is the lesson we learn from nature—*how* it will be we are not meant to know. There is an old Greek saying to the effect, to try to know what the gods did not tell us, is not piety. If God wished us to know what is to be, He would tell us. Darwin has shown us that there is continuity from beginning to end.   *Ibid.*

I believe in the continuity of Self. If there were an annihilation or complete change of our individual self-consciousness we might become somebody else, but we should not be ourselves. Personally, I have no doubt of the persistence of the individual after death, as we call it. I cannot imagine the very crown and flower of creation being destroyed by its author. I do not say it is impossible, it is not for us to say either yes or no; we have simply to trust, but that trust or faith is implanted in us, and is strengthened by everything around us.

          Ibid.

Do we really lose those who are called before us? I feel that they are even nearer to us than when they were with us in life. We must take a larger view. Our life does not end here, if only we can see that our horizon here is but like a curtain that separates us from what is beyond. Those who go before us are beyond our horizon at present, but we have no right to suppose that they have completely vanished. We cannot see them, that is all. And even that, we know, can last for a short time only. We have lived and done our work in life, before we knew those we loved, and we may have to live the same number of years separated from them. But nothing can be lost: it depends on ourselves to keep those we loved always near to our thoughts, even though our eyes look in vain for them. The world is larger than this little earth, our thoughts go further than this short life, and if we can but find our home in this larger world, we shall find that this larger home is full of those whom we loved, and who loved us. There is no *chance* in life; a few years more, a few years less, will seem as nothing to us hereafter.   *Ibid.*

I fully take in the real death (of my child), I know I shall follow and die the same real death, and through that same real death I trust the spirit of Christ will be my guide and helper, and bring me to a better life, and unite me again with those whom I have loved, and whom I love still, and those who have loved me and love me still. God is no giver of imperfect gifts, and He has given me life, but life on earth is imperfect. He has given me love, but love on earth is imperfect. I believe, I must believe in perfection, and therefore I believe in a life perfected, and in a love perfected. *"Hier stehe ich, ich kann nicht anders —Gott helfe mir, Amen."*   *MS.*

It seems hard, it seems so unintelligible, so far above us, that we should know nothing at all of what is to come—that we should be so completely separated for a time from those whom we love. Whence all these limits ? Whence all those desires in us that cannot be fulfilled ? The limits teach us one lesson, that we are in the hands of a Higher Power. Wonderful as our body and our senses are, they are a prison and chains, and they could not be meant for anything else.   *MS.*

Of what is to come, what is in store for us, we know nothing, and the more we know that, the greater and stronger our faith. It must be right, it cannot be wrong. Why was the past often so beautiful ? Because all tends to beauty, to perfection, and the highest point of perfection is love. We are far from that here, yet all the miseries of this life, or many at least, would vanish before love. Life seems most unnatural in what we call the most highly civilised countries—the struggle of life is fiercest there. Rest and love seem impossible, and yet that is what we are yearning for, and it may be granted us hereafter.   *MS.*

How is it that we know so little of life after death—that we can hardly imagine anything without feeling that it is all human poetry ? We are to believe the best, but nothing definite, nothing that can be described. It is the same with God, we are to believe the best we can believe, and yet all is earthly, human, weak. We are in a dark prison here; let us believe that outside it there is no darkness but light—but what light, who knows ?   *MS.*

Wait, wait, do not ask. Children ask every year what the Christ Child will bring them, but they are not told, they wait in the dark room.

Every year they expect something quite new, but it is always the same old Christmas Tree, with its lights and flowers, and all the rest. And why should it be so different when the door opens, and we step out of this dark life into the bright room? Why should all be different? We have stepped into this dark room here on earth, and how often did we think it was very bright, and very warm. We shall step into another room, and it will be brighter, warmer, more pure, more perfect.

MS.

What is past, present, future? Is it not all one—only the past and the future somewhere where at present we cannot be? Wait a little time, and the eternal will take place of the present—and we shall have the past again—for the past is not lost. Nothing is lost—but this waiting is sometimes very hard, and this longing very hard. Friends go on all sides, it seems a different world, yet there is work to do, and there is much left to love.

MS.

If immortality is meant for no more than a continuance of existence, if by a belief in immortality on the part of the Jews is meant no more than that the Jews did not believe in the annihilation of the soul at the time of death, we may confidently assert that, to the bulk of the Jewish nation, this very idea of annihilation was as yet unfamiliar.   The fact is that the idea of absolute annihilation and nothingness is hardly ever found except among people whose mind has received some amount of philosophical education, certainly more than what the Jews possessed in early times.   The Jews did not believe in the utter destruction of the soul, but, on the other hand, their idea of life after death was hardly that of life at all.   It was existence without life.   Death was considered by them, as by the Greeks, as the greatest of misfortunes.   To rejoice in death is a purely Christian, not a Jewish, idea.   Though the Jews believed that the souls continued to exist in Sheol, they did not believe that the wicked would there be punished and the good rewarded. All rewards and punishments for virtue or vice were confined to this world, and a long life was regarded as a sure proof of the favour of Jehovah. It was the Jewish conception of God, as infinitely removed from this world, that made a belief in true immortality almost impossible for them, and excluded all hope for a nearer approach to God, or for any share in that true immortality which belonged to Him and to Him alone.

Gifford Lectures, III.

Our angels live in heaven, not on earth. We
only recognise the angelic in man, even in those
we love the most, when we can no longer see them.
They are then nearer us than ever, we love them
more than ever. Happy are those who have such
angels in heaven, who draw our hearts away from
earth and fill them with longing for our true
home. They lighten the burden of life, they give a
quiet, gentle tone to the joys of life, and they teach
us to love those who are left to us on earth, it may
be but for a few days or years, with a love which we
never knew before, a love which bears all things,
believes all things, and gladly pardons all things.

MS.

Life eternal. Why do we so seldom face the
great problem ?   With me the chief reason was
the conviction that we can *know* nothing—that
we must wait and trust—do our work for the day
which is—and believe that nothing can happen
to us unless God wills it. Know, where knowledge is
possible; believe, trust, where faith only is possible.

MS.

I know we shall meet again, for God does not
destroy what He has made, nor do souls meet by
accident. This life is full of riddles, but divine
riddles have a divine solution.   *Life.*

THE INFINITE

THOUGH we cannot know things finite, as they are in themselves, we know at all events that they are. And this applies to our perception of the Infinite also. We do not know through our senses what it is, but we know through our very senses that it is. We feel the pressure of the Infinite in the Finite, and unless we had that feeling, we should have no true and safe foundation for whatever we may afterward believe of the Infinite. Some critics have urged that what I call the Infinite . . . is the Indefinite only. Of course it is. . . . We can know the Infinite as the Indefinite only, or as the partially defined. We try to define it, and to know it more and more, but we never finish it. The whole history of religion represents the continuous progress of the human definition of the Infinite, but however far that definition may advance, it will never exhaust the Infinite. Could we define it all, it would cease to be the Infinite, it would cease to be the Unknown, it would cease to be the Inconceivable or the Divine .

Chips from a German Workshop.

What we feel through the pressure on all our senses is the pressure of the Infinite. Our senses, if I may say so, feel nothing but the Infinite, and out of that plenitude they apprehend the Finite. To apprehend the Finite is the same as to define the Infinite.   *Ibid.*

We accept the primitive savage with nothing but his five senses. These five senses supply him with a knowledge of finite things; the problem is how such a being ever comes to think or speak of anything not finite, but infinite. It is his senses which give him the first impression of infinite things and force him to the admission of the Infinite. Everything of which his senses cannot perceive a limit is to a primitive savage, or to any man in an early stage of intellectual activity, unlimited or infinite. Man sees to a certain point; and there his eyesight breaks down. But exactly where his eyesight breaks down there presses upon him, whether he likes it or not, the perception of the unlimited, or infinite. It may be said this is not perception, in the ordinary sense of the word. No more it is, but still less is it mere reasoning. In perceiving the Infinite, we neither count, nor measure, nor compare, nor name. We know not what it is, but we know that it is, and we know it because we actually feel it and are brought in contact with it.   If it seems too bold to say that man actually sees the invisible let us say that he suffers from the invisible, and this invisible is only a special name for the Infinite.   The Infinite, therefore, instead of being merely a late abstraction is really implied in the earliest manifestations of our sensuous knowledge.   It was true from the very first, but it was not yet defined or named. If the Infinite had not from the very first been present in our sensuous perceptions, such a word as infinite would be a sound and nothing else. With very finite perception there is a concomitant perception or a concomitant sentiment or present- ment of the Infinite; from the very first act of touch, or hearing, at sight, we are brought in contact, not only with the visible, but also at the same time with an invisible universe.   We have in this that without which no religion would have been possi- ble; we have in that perception of the Infinite the root of the whole historical development of re- ligion.   *Hibbert Lectures.*

No thought, no name is ever entirely lost. When we here in this ancient Abbey,* which was built on the ruins of a still more ancient **Roman**

* Westminster.

temple, seek for a name for the invisible, the
Infinite that surrounds us on every side, the
unknown, the true Self of the world, and the true
Self of ourselves—we, too, feeling once more like
children, kneeling in a small dark room, can hardly
find a better name than, "Our Father, which art
in Heaven."   *Ibid.*

The idea of the Infinite, which is at the root of all
religious thought, is not simply evolved by reason
out of nothing, but supplied to us, in its original
form, by our senses. Beyond, behind, beneath
and within the Finite, the Infinite is always present
to our senses. It presses upon us, it grows upon us
from every side. What we call finite in space and
time, in form and word, is nothing but a veil or
a net which we ourselves have thrown over the
infinite. The Finite by itself, without the Infinite,
is simply inconceivable; as inconceivable as the
Infinite without the Finite. As reason deals with
the finite materials, supplied to us by our senses,
faith, or whatever else we like to call it, deals
with the Infinite that underlies the Finite. What
we call sense, reason, and faith, are three functions
of one and the same perceptive self; but without
sense, both reason and faith are impossible, at
least to human beings like ourselves. *Ibid.*

The ancestors of our race did not only believe
in divine powers more or less manifest to their
senses, in rivers and mountains, in the sky and the
sun, in the thunder and rain, but their senses
likewise suggested to them two of the most essential
elements of all religion, the concept of the infinite,
and the concept of law and order, as revealed
before them, the one in the golden sea behind the
dawn, the other in the daily path of the sun. . . .
These two concepts which sooner or later must be
taken in and minded by every human being, were
at first no more than an impulse, but their impulsive
force would not rest till it had beaten into the
minds of the fathers of our race the deep and
indelible impression that "all is right," and
filled them with a hope, and more than a hope,
that "all will be right."   *Ibid.*

The real religious instinct or impulse is the
perception of the Infinite.   *Ibid.*

All objects which we perceive and afterward
conceive and name must be circumscribed, must
have been separated from their surroundings,
must be measurable, and can thus only become
perceivable and knowable and nameable. . . .

They are therefore finite in their very nature.
. . . If finiteness is a necessary characteristic
of our ordinary knowledge, it requires but little
reflection to perceive that limitation or finiteness,
in whatever sense we use it, always implies a
something beyond. We are told that our mind is
so constituted, whether it is our fault or not, that
we cannot conceive an absolute limit. Beyond
every limit we must always take it for granted
that there is something else. But what is the
reason of this? The reason why we cannot conceive an absolute limit is because we never perceive
an absolute limit; or, in other words, because in
perceiving the finite, we always perceive the Infinite
also. . . . There is no limit which has not
two sides, the one turned toward us, the other
turned toward what is beyond; and it is that
Beyond which from the earliest days has formed
the only real foundation of all that we call transcendental in our perceptual, as well as in our
conceptual, knowledge. *Gifford Lectures, I.*

The Infinite was not discovered behind the veil
of nature only, though its manifestation in physical
phenomena was no doubt the most primitive and
the most fertile source of mythological and religious
ideas. There were two more manifestations of the

Infinite and the unknown, which must not be neglected, if we wish to gain a complete insight into
the theogonic process through which the human
mind had to pass from its earliest days. The
Infinite disclosed itself not only in nature but likewise in man, looked upon as an object, and lastly
in man looked upon as a subject. Man looked
upon as an object, as a living thing, was felt to be
more than a mere part of nature. There was
something in man, whether it was called breath or
spirit or soul or mind, which was perceived and
yet not perceived, which was behind the veil of
the body, and from a very early time was believed
to remain free from decay, even when illness and
death had destroyed the body in which it seemed
to dwell. There was nothing to force even the
simplest peasant to believe that because he saw
his father dead, and his body decaying, therefore
what was known as the man himself, call it his
soul or his mind, or his person, had vanished
altogether out of existence. A philosopher may
arrive at such an idea, but a man of ordinary
understanding, though terrified by the aspect of
death, would rather be inclined to believe that
what he had known and loved and called his
father or mother, must be somewhere, though no
longer in the body. . . . It is perhaps too
much to say that such a belief was universal; but

it certainly was and is still very widely spread. In fact it constitutes a very large portion of religion, and religious worship. *Ibid.*

Nature, Man, and Self are the three great manifestations in which the Infinite in some shape or other has been perceived, and every one of these perceptions has in its historical development contributed to what may be called religion.

Ibid.

Like all other experiences, our religious experience begins with the senses. Though the senses seem to deliver to us finite experiences only, many if not all, of them can be shown to involve something beyond the known, something unknown, something which I claim the liberty to call infinite. In this way the human mind was led to the recognition of undefined, infinite agents or agencies beyond, behind, and within our finite experience. The feelings of fear, awe, reverence, and love excited by the manifestations of some of these agents or powers began to react on the human mind, and thus produced what we call Natural Religion in its lowest and simplest form—fear, awe, reverence, and love of the gods. *Ibid.*

The perception of the Infinite can be shown by historical evidence to be the one element shared in common by all religions. Only we must not forget that, like every other concept, that of the Infinite also had to pass through many phases in its historical evolution, beginning with the simple negation of what is finite, and the assertion of an invisible Beyond, and leading up to a perceptive belief in that most real Infinite in which we live and move and have our being.

Gifford Lectures, IV.

KNOWLEDGE

THE lesson that there are limits to our knowledge is an old lesson, but it has to be taught again and again. It was taught by Buddha, it was taught by Socrates, and it was taught for the last time in the most powerful manner by Kant. Philosophy has been called the knowledge of our knowledge; it might be called more truly the knowledge of our ignorance, or, to adopt the more moderate language of Kant, the knowledge of the limits of our knowledge. *Last Essays.*

Metaphysical truth is wider than physical truth, and the new discoveries of physical observers, if they are to be more than merely contingent truths, must find their appointed place and natural refuge within the immovable limits traced by the metaphysician. . . . It is only after having mastered the principles of metaphysics that the student of nature can begin his work in the right spirit, knowing the horizon of human knowledge, and guided by principles as unchangeable as the pole star. *Ibid.*

There is no subject in the whole realm of human knowledge that cannot be rendered clear and intelligible, if we ourselves have perfectly mastered it.
Chips from a German Workshop.

The bridge of thoughts and sighs that spans the whole history of the Aryan world has its first arch in the Veda, its last in Kant's "Critique of Pure Reason." In the Veda we watch the first unfolding of the human mind as we can watch it nowhere else. Life seems simple, natural, childlike. . . . What is beneath, and above, and beyond this life is dimly perceived, and expressed in a thousand words and ways, all mere stammerings, all aiming to express what cannot be expressed, yet all full of a belief in the real presence of the Divine in Nature, of the Infinite in the Finite. . . . While in the Veda we may study the childhood, we may study in Kant's "Critique" the perfect manhood of the Aryan mind. It has passed through many phases, and every one of them . . . has left its mark. It is no longer dogmatical, no longer sceptical, least of all is it positive. . . . It stands before us conscious of its weakness and its strength, modest yet brave. It knows what the old idols of its childhood and youth were made of. It does not break them, it only tries to understand

them, but it places above them the Ideals of
Reason—no longer tangible—not even within the
reach of the understanding—but real—bright and
heavenly stars to guide us even in the darkest night.
Translation of Kant's "Critique of Pure Reason."

All knowledge, in order to be knowledge, must
pass through two gates, and two gates only; the
gate of the senses, and the gate of reason. Religious knowledge also, whether true or false, must
have passed through these two gates. At these
two gates therefore we take our stand. Whatever
claims to have entered in by any other gate,
whether that gate is called primeval revelation or
religious instinct, must be rejected as contraband
of thought; and whatever claims to have entered
by the gate of reason, without having first passed
through the gate of the senses, must equally be
rejected, as without sufficient warrant, or ordered
at least to go back to the first gate, in order to
produce there its full credentials.

Hibbert Lectures.

LANGUAGE

THE history of language opens a vista which makes one feel almost giddy if one tries to see the end of it, but the measuring rod of the chronologist seems to me entirely out of place. Those who have eyes to see will see the immeasurable distance between the first historical appearance of language and the real beginnings of human speech; those who cannot see will oscillate between the wildly large figures of the Buddhists, or the wildly small figures of the Rabbis, but they will never lay hold of what by its very nature is indefinite.   *Life.*

By no effort of the understanding, by no stretch of imagination, can I explain to myself how language could have grown out of anything which animals possess, even if we granted them millions of years for that purpose. If anything has a right to the name of specific difference, it is language, as we find it in man, and in man only. Even if we removed the name of specific difference from our philosophic dictionaries, I should still hold that

nothing deserves the name of man except what is
able to speak. *Science of Thought.*

Every language has to be learned, but who made
the language that was to be learned ? It matters
little whether we call language an instinct, a gift, a
talent, a faculty, or the *proprium* of man; certain
it is that neither language, nor the power
of language, nor the conditions under which
alone language can exist, are to be discovered
anywhere in the whole animal kingdom, except
in man. *Ibid.*

It was Christianity which first broke down the
barrier between Jew and Gentile, between Greek
and Barbarian, between the white and the black.
Humanity is a word which you look for in vain in
Plato and Aristotle; the idea of mankind as one
family, as the children of one God, is an idea of
Christian growth; and the science of mankind,
and of the languages of mankind, is a science which,
without Christianity, would never have sprung
into life. When people had been taught to look
upon all men as brethren, then, and then only, did
the variety of human speech present itself as a
problem that called for a solution in the eyes of

thoughtful observers; and from an historical point
of view it is not too much to say that the first day
of Pentecost marks the real beginning of the science
of language.   *Science of Language.*

And now, if we gaze from our native shores over
the vast ocean of human speech, with its waves
rolling on from continent to continent, rising under
the fresh breezes of the morning of history, and
slowly heaving in our own more sultry atmosphere,
with sails gliding over its surface, and many an
oar ploughing through its surf, and the flags of all
nations waving joyously together, with its rocks
and wrecks, its storms and battles, yet reflecting
serenely all that is beneath and above and around
it; if we gaze and hearken to the strange sounds
rushing past our ears in unbroken strains, it seems
no longer a wild tumult, but we feel as if placed
within some ancient cathedral, listening to a chorus
of innumerable voices: and the more intensely we
listen, the more all discords melt away into higher
harmonies, till at last we hear but one majestic tri-
chord, or a mighty unison, as at the end of a sacred
symphony. Such visions will float through the study
of the grammarian, and in the midst of toilsome
researches his heart will suddenly beat, as he feels
the conviction growing upon him that men are

brethren in the simplest sense of the word—the children of the same Father—whatever their country, their language, and their faith.

Bunsen's "Philosophy of Universal History," I.

LIFE

ALL really great and honest men may be said to live three lives: there is one life which is seen and accepted by the world at large, a man's outward life; there is a second life which is seen by a man's most intimate friends, his household life; and there is a third life, seen only by the man himself, and by Him who searcheth the heart, which may be called the inner or heavenly—a life led in communion with God, a life of aspiration rather than of fulfilment. *Chips from a German Workshop.*

Where Plato could only see imperfections, the failures of the founders of human speech, we see, as everywhere else in human life, a natural progress from the imperfect toward the perfect, unceasing attempts at realising the ideal, and the frequent triumphs of the human mind over the inevitable difficulties of this earthly condition—difficulties not of man's own making, but, as I firmly believe, prepared for him, and not without a purpose, as toils and tasks, by a higher Power, and by the highest Wisdom. *Ibid.*

Our life is not completely in our hands—we must submit to many things which we may smile at in our inmost heart, but which nevertheless are essential, not only to our happiness, but to our fulfilling the duties which we are called to fulfil. We ought to look upon the circumstances in which we are born and brought up as ordained by a Higher Power, and we must learn to walk the path which is pointed out to us!   *Life.*

It is difficult to be always true to ourselves, to be always what we wish to be, what we feel we ought to be. As long as we feel that, as long as we do not surrender the ideal of our life, all is right. Our aspirations represent the true nature of our soul much more than our everyday life. I feel as much as you, how far I have been left behind in the race which I meant to run, but I honestly try to rouse myself, and to live up to what I feel I ought to be. Let us keep up our constant fight against all that is small and common and selfish, let us never lose our faith in the ideal life, in what we ought to be, and in what with constant prayer to God we shall be, and let us never forget how unworthy we are of all the blessings God has showered down upon us.   *Ibid.*

I feel quite thankful for any little misfortune; it is like paying something of the large debt of happiness we owe, though it is but a very trifling interest, and the capital we must owe forever.   *MS.*

I thought a long time about my happiness, and my unworthiness, and God's unbounded mercy. And then I heard the words within me: "Be not afraid." Yes, there must be no fear. Where there is fear, there is no perfect love. Our happiness here is but a foretaste of our blessed life hereafter. We must never forget that. We shall be called away, but we shall meet again.   *MS.*

I begin to be quite thankful for my disappointment—we all want winding up, and nothing does it so well as a great disappointment, if we only see clearly Who sent it and then forget everything else.   *MS.*

One sometimes forgets that all this is only the preparation for what is to come hereafter. Yet we should never forget this, otherwise this life loses its true meaning and purpose. If we only know what we live for here, we can easily find out what is worth having in this life, and what is not; we can easily go on without many things which others, whose eyes are fixed on this world only, consider essential to their happiness.   *MS.*

The spirit of love, and the spirit of truth, are the two life springs of our whole being—or, what is the same, of our whole religion.   If we lose that bond, which holds us and binds us to a higher world, our life becomes purposeless, joyless; if it holds us and supports, life becomes perfect, all little cares vanish, and we feel we are working out a great purpose, as well as we can, a purpose not our own, not selfish, not self-seeking, but, in the truest sense of the word, God serving and God seeking. . . . Gentleness is a kind of mixture of love and truthfulness, and it should be the highest object of our life to attain more and more to that true gentleness which throws such a charm over all our life.   There is a gentleness of voice, of look, of movement, of speech, all of which are but the expressions of true gentleness of heart.

MS.

It is impossible to take too high a view of life; the very highest we take is still too low.   One feels that more and more as our life draws to its close, and many things that seemed important once are seen to be of no consequence, while only a few things remain which will tell forever. *MS*.

I don't believe in what is called worldly wisdom. I do not think the world was made for it—with real faith in a higher life I believe one can pass through this life without let or hindrance. What I dread are compromises. There are false notes in them always, and a false note goes on forever. *MS*.

How thankful we ought to be every minute of our existence to Him who gives us all richly to enjoy. How little one has deserved this happy life, much less than many poor sufferers to whom life is a burden and a hard and bitter trial. But then, how much greater the claims on us; how much more sacred the duty never to trifle, never to waste time and power, never to compromise, but to live in all things, small and great, to the praise and glory of God, to have God always present with us, and to be ready to follow His voice, and His voice only. Has our prosperity taught us to meet adversity when it comes? I often tremble, but then I commit all to God, and I say, "Have mercy upon me, a miserable sinner." *Life*.

There is something very awful in this life, and it is not right to try to forget it. It is well to be reminded by the trials of others of what may befall us, and what is kept from us only by the love of our Father in Heaven, not by any merit of our own.   *MS.*

How different life is to what one thought it when young, how all around us falls together, till we ourselves fall together. How meaningless and vain everything seems on earth, and how closely the reality of the life beyond approaches us. Many days were beautiful here, but the greater the happiness the more bitter the thought that it all passes away, that nothing remains of earthly happiness, but a grateful heart and faith in God who knows best what is best for us.   *MS.*

Oh! if we could even in this life forget all that is unessential, all that makes it so hard for us to recognise true greatness and goodness in the character of those with whom this life brings us in contact for a little while! How much we lose by making little things so important, and how rarely do we think highly enough of what is essential and lasting!
                    MS.

You must accustom yourself more and more to the thought that here is not our abiding city, that all that we call ours here is only lent, not given us, and that if the sorrow for those we have lost remains the same, we must yet acknowledge with gratitude to God the great blessing of having enjoyed so many years with those whom He gave us, as parents, or children, or friends. One forgets so easily the happy years one has had with those who were the nearest to us. Even these years of happiness, however short they may have been, were only given us; we had not deserved them. I know well there is no comfort for this pain of parting: the wound always remains, but one learns to bear the pain, and learns to thank God for what He gave, for the beautiful memories of the past, and the yet more beautiful hope for the future. If a man has lent us anything for several years, and at last takes it back, he expects gratitude, not anger, and if God has more patience with our weakness than men have, yet murmurs and complaints for the life which He measured out for us as is best for us are not what He expected from us. A spirit of resignation to God's will is our only comfort, the only relief under the trials God lays upon us, and with such a spirit the heaviest as well as the lightest trials of life are not only bearable, but useful, and gratitude to God, and joy in life and death remain untroubled.   *Life.*

By a grave one learns what life really is—that it is not here but elsewhere—that this is the exile and there is our home. As we grow older the train of life goes faster and faster, those with whom we travelled together step out from station to station, and our own station too will soon be marked.

MS.

It seems to me so ungrateful to allow one moment to pass that is not full of joy and happiness, and devotion to Him who gives us all this richly to enjoy. The clouds will come, they must come, but they ought never to be of our own making.

Life.

The shadows fall thicker and thicker, but even in the shade it is well, often better than in full sunshine. And when the evening comes, one is tired, and ready to sleep! And so all is ordered for us, if we only accommodate ourselves to it quietly.

Ibid.

As long as God wills it we must learn to bear this life, but when He calls us we willingly close our eyes, for we know it is better for us there than here. When so many whom we loved are gone before us, we follow gladly; and the older we become here, the more one feels that death is a relief. And yet we can thankfully enjoy what is still left us on earth, even if our hearts no longer cling to it as formerly.

Ibid.

Our life here is not our own work, and we know that it is best for us all just as it is. We ought to bear it, and we must bear it; and the more patiently, yes, the more joyfully, we accommodate ourselves to it, the better for us. We must take life as it is, as the way appointed for us, and that must lead to a certain goal. Some go sooner, some later, but we all go the same way, and all find the same place of rest. Impatience, gloom, murmurs and tears do not help us, do not alter anything and make the road longer, not shorter. Quiet, resignation, thankfulness and faith help us forward, and alone make it possible to perform the duties which we all, each in his own sphere, have to fulfil. . . . The darker the night, the clearer the stars in heaven.   *Ibid.*

How different life might be, if in our daily intercourse and conversation we thought of our

friends as lying before us on the last bed of flowers
—how differently we should then judge, and how
differently we should act.   All that is of the earth
is then forgotten, all the little failings inherent in
human nature vanish from our minds, and we
only see what was good, unselfish and loving in
that soul, and we think with regret of how much
more we might have done to requite that love.   It
is curious how forgetful we are of death, how little
we think that we are dying daily, and that what
we call life is really death, and death the beginning
of a higher life.   Such a thought should not make
our life less bright, but rather more—it should
make us feel how unimportant many things are
which we consider all-important: how much we
could bear which we think unbearable, if only we
thought that to-morrow we ourselves or our
friends may be taken away, at least for a time.
You should think of death, should feel that what
you call your own is only lent to you, and that all
that remains as a real comfort is the good work
done in this short journey, the true unselfish love
shewn to those whom God has given us, has
placed near to us, not without a high purpose.

Ibid.

What a marvel life seems to be the older we
grow! So far from becoming more intelligible, it

becomes a greater wonder every day. One
stands amazed, and everything seems so small—
the little one can do so very small. One ought
not to brood too much, when there is no chance of
light, and yet how natural it is that one should
brood over life and death, rather than on the little
things of life.   *Ibid.*

If we only hold fast the belief that nothing
happens but by the will of God, we learn to be
still and can bear everything. The older one
grows, the more one feels sure that life here is but
a long imprisonment, and one longs for freedom
and higher efforts. . . . How small and insignificant is all in this life when we rise our eyes
above. Gazing up to the Lord of the Universe,
all strife is made easy. We speak different tongues
when we think of the Highest, but we all mean
the same thing.   *MS.*

It is sad to think of all that was and is no more,
and yet there is something much more real in
memory than one used to think. All is there but
what our weak human senses require, and nothing
is lost, nothing can be lost except what we know
would vanish one day, but what was the husk only,

not the kernel. I have learned to live with those who went before us, and they seem more entirely our own than when they were with us in the body. And as long as we have duties to fulfil, so long as there are others who lean on us and want us, life can be lived a few years longer; it can only be a few years. *MS.*

Life is earnest! is a very old lesson, and we are never too old to learn it. "Life is an art," is Goethe's doctrine, and there is some truth in it also, as long as art does not imply artful or artificial. Huxley used to say the highest end of life is action, not knowledge. There I quite differ. First knowledge, then action, and what a lottery action is! The best intentions often fail, and what is done to-day is undone to-morrow. However, we must toil on and do what every day brings us, and do it as well as we can, and better, if possible, than anybody else. *Life.*

What can we call ours if God did not vouchsafe it to us from day to day? Yet it is so difficult to give oneself up entirely to Him, to trust everything to His Love and Wisdom. I thought I could say, "Thy Will be done," but I found I could not: my own will struggled against His Will. I prayed as we ought not to pray, and yet He heard me.   It is so difficult not to grow very fond of this life and all its happiness, but the more we love it, the more we suffer, for we know we must lose it and it must all pass away.   *MS.*

Our idea of life grows larger, and birth and death seem but like morning and evening.   One feels that as it has been so it will be again, and all one can do is to try to make the best of every day, as it comes and goes.   *Life.*

The things that annoy us in life are after all very trifling things, if we always bear in mind for what purpose we are here.   And even in the heavier trials, one knows, or one should know, that all is sent by a higher power, and in the end must be for our best interests.   It is true we cannot understand it, but we can understand that God rules in the world in the smallest and in the largest events, and he who keeps that ever in mind has the peace of God, and enjoys his life as long as it lasts.

                                              Ibid.

Life may grow more strange and awful every day, but the more strange and awful it grows, the more it reveals to us its truest meaning and reality, and the deepest depth of its divinity. "And God saw everything that He had made, and behold, it was very good."   *Ibid.*

Enjoy the precious years God has added to your life, with constant gratitude, with quiet and purity of soul, looking more to the heavenly than to the earthly; that gives true joyfulness of soul, if we *every moment* recollect what is eternal, and never quite lose ourselves in the small, or even the large cares of life.

                                                    Ibid.

If we live on this earth only, if our thoughts are hemmed in by the narrow horizon of this life, then we lose indeed those whom death takes from us. But it is death itself which teaches us that there is a Beyond, we are lifted up and see a new world, far beyond what we had seen before. In that wide world we lead a new and larger life, a life which includes those we no longer see on earth, but whom we cannot surrender. The old Indian philosophers say that no one can find the truth whose heart is attached to his wife and children. No doubt perfect freedom from all affections would make life and death very easy. But may not the very love which we feel for those who belong to us,

even when they are taken from us, bring light to
our eyes, and make us see the truth that, by that
very love, we belong to another world, and that
from that world, however little we can here know
about it, love will not be excluded. We believe what
we desire—true—but why do we desire? Let us be
ourselves, let us be what we were meant to be on
earth, and trust to Him who made us what we are.

MS.

Yes, every day adds a new thin layer of new
thoughts, and these layers form the texture of our
character. The materials come floating toward
us, but the way in which they settle down depends
much on the ebb and flow within us. We can do
much to keep off foreign elements, and to attach
and retain those which serve best in building up a
strong rock. But from time to time a great sorrow
breaks through all the strata of our soul—all is
upheaved, shattered, distorted. In nature all that is
grand dates from such convulsions—why should we
wish for a new smooth surface, or let our sorrows
be covered by the flat sediment of everyday life?

MS.

If we feel that this life can only be a link in a
chain without beginning and without end, in a
circle which has its beginning and its end every-

where and nowhere, we learn to bear it, and to enjoy it too, in a new sense. What we achieve here assumes a new meaning—it will not altogether perish, whether for good or for evil. What is done in time is done forever—what is done by one affects us all. Thus our love too is not lost— what is loved in time is loved forever. The form changes, but that which changes, which undergoes change, remains itself unchanged. We seem to love the fleeting forms of life—and yet how can we truly love what is so faithless? No, we truly love what is, and was, and will be, hidden under the fleeting forms of life, but in itself more than those fleeting forms, however fair. We love the fair appearance too—how could it be otherwise? But we should love them only as belonging to what we love—not as being what we love. So it is, or, rather, so it ought to be. Yet while we are what we are, we love the flower, not the sightless grain of seed, and when that flower fades and passes away, we mourn for it, and our only comfort is that we too fade and pass away. Then we follow there, wherever they go. Some flowers fade sooner, some later, but none is quite forgotten.

MS.

It would be difficult to say at what moment in our young lives real responsibility begins. The law fixes a time, our own heart cannot do that. Yet in spite of this unknown quantity at the beginning, we begin afterward to reckon with ourselves. Why should we protest against a similar unknown quantity before the beginning of our life on earth? Wherever and whenever it was, we feel that we have made ourselves what we are. Is not that a useful article of faith? Does it not help us to decide on undoing what we have done wrong and in doing all the good we can, even if it does not bear fruit, within or without, in this life? A break of consciousness does not seem incompatible with a sense of responsibility, if we know by reasoning though not by recollection that what we see done in ourselves must have been done by ourselves. And even if we waive the question of responsibility for the first two or three years of our life on earth, surely we existed during those years though we do not recollect it—then why not before our life on earth?   *MS.*

We must learn to live two lives—this short life here on earth with its joys and sorrows, and that true life beyond, of which this is only a fragment, or an interruption. When we enter into that true life, we shall find what we cannot find here, we shall find what we have lost here. If only so many things did not seem so irregular, so unnatural. The death of young children before their parents. We love them better because we know we can lose them—that is true—but yet it is a hard lesson to learn. *MS.*

One month will go after another, till at last this journey is over, and we look back on it grateful for the many pleasures it has given us, grateful for the company of so many kind friends whom we met, grateful also for the struggles which we had to go through and which will appear so small, and so little worth our tears and anguish, when all is over and the last station and resting place reached in safety. *MS.*

LOVE

I CANNOT help thinking that the souls toward whom we feel drawn in this life are the very souls whom we knew and loved in a former life, and that the souls who repel us here, we do not know why, are the souls that earned our disapproval, the souls from whom we kept aloof, in a former life. But let us remember that if our love is the love of what is merely phenomenal, the love of the body, the kindness of the heart, the vigour and wisdom of the intellect, our love is the love of changing and perishable things. . . . But if our love, under all its earthly aspects, was the love of the true soul, of what is immortal and divine in every man and woman, that love cannot die, but will find once more what seems beautiful, true and lovable in worlds to come, as in worlds that have passed. . . . What we truly love in everything is the eternal *âtman*, the immortal self, and as we should add, the immortal God, for the immortal self and the immortal God must be one.

Last Essays.

We must not forget that if earthly love has in the vulgar mind been often degraded into mere animal passion, it still remains in its purest sense the highest mystery of our existence, the most perfect blessing and delight on earth, and at the same time the truest pledge of our more than human nature. To be able to feel the same unselfish devotion to the Deity which the human heart is capable of, if filled with love for another human soul, is something that may well be called the best religion.   *Gifford Lectures, IV.*

What the present generation ought to learn, the young as well as the old, is spirit and perseverance to discover the beautiful, pleasure and joy in making it known, and resigning ourselves with grateful hearts to its enjoyment; in a word—love, in the old, true, eternal meaning of the word. Only sweep away the dust of self-conceit, the cobwebs of selfishness, the mud of envy, and the old type of humanity will soon reappear, as it was when it could still "embrace millions." The love of mankind, the true fountain of all humanity, is still there; it can never be quite choked up. He who can descend into this fountain of youth, who can again recover himself, who can again be that which he was by nature, loves the beautiful wherever he finds it; he understands enjoyment and enthusiasm, in the few quiet hours which he can win for himself in the noisy, deafening hurry of the times in which we live.

Chips from a German Workshop.

Would not the carrying out of one single commandment of Christ, "Love one another," change the whole aspect of the world, and sweep away prisons and workhouses, and envying and strife, and all the strongholds of the devil? Two thousand years have nearly passed and people have not yet understood that one single command of Christ, "Love one another"! We are as perfect heathens in that one respect as it is possible to be. No, this world might be heaven on earth, if we would but carry out God's work and God's commandments, and so it will be hereafter.   *Life.*

If we do a thing because we think it is our duty, we generally fail; that is the old law which makes slaves of us. The real spirng of our life, and of our work in life, must be love—true deep love— not love of this or that person, or for this or that reason, but deep human love, devotion of soul to soul, love of God realised where alone it can be, in love of those whom He loves. Everything else is weak, passes away; that love alone supports us, makes life tolerable, binds the present together with the past and future, and is, we may trust, imperishable.   *Ibid.*

Love which seems so unselfish may become very selfish if we are not on our guard. Do not shut your eyes to what is dark in others, but do not dwell on it except so far as it helps to bring out more strongly what is bright in them, lovely and unselfish. The true happiness of true love is self forgetfulness and trust.   *Ibid.*

There is nothing in life like a mother's love, though children often do not find it out till it is too late. If you want to be really happy in life, love your mother with all your heart; it is a blessing to feel that you belong to her, and that through her you are connected by an unbroken chain with the highest source of our being.   *MS.*

Is there such a thing as a lost love? I do not believe it. Nothing that is true and great is ever lost on earth, though its fulfilment may be deferred beyond this short life. . . . Love is eternal, and all the more so if it does not meet with its fulfilment on earth. If once we know that our lives are in the hands of God, and that nothing can happen to us without His Will, we are thankful for the trials which He sends us. Is there anyone who loves us more than God? anyone who knows better what is for our real good than God? This little artificial and complicated society of ours may sometimes seem to be outside His control, but if we think so it is our own fault, and we have to suffer for it. We blame our friends, we mistrust ourselves, and all this because our wild hearts will not be quiet in that narrow cage in which they must be kept to prevent mischief. *Life.*

Does love pass away (with death)? I cannot believe it. God made us as we are, many, instead of one. Christ died for all of us individually, and such as we are—beings incomplete in themselves, and perfect only through love to God on one side, and through love to man on the other. We want both kinds of love for our very existence, and therefore in a higher and better existence too the love of kindred souls may well exist together with our love of God. We need not love those we love best on earth less in heaven, though we may love all better than we do on earth. After all, love seems only the taking away those unnatural barriers which divide us from our fellow creatures—it is only the restoration of that union which binds us all together in God, and which has been broken on earth we know not how. In Christ alone that union was preserved, for He loved us *all* with a love warmer than the love of a husband for his wife, or a mother for her child. He gave His life for us, and if we ask ourselves there is hardly a husband or a mother who would really suffer death for his wife or her child. Thus we see that even what seems to us the most perfect love is very far as yet from the perfection of love which drives out the whole self and all that is selfish, and we must try to love more, not to love less, and trust that what is imperfect here is not meant to be destroyed, but to be made perfect hereafter. With God nothing is imperfect. We must live and love in God, and then we need not fear: though our life seem chequered and fleeting, we know that there is a home for us in God, and rest for all our troubles in Christ. *Ibid.*

Let us hold together while life lasts. Hand in hand we may achieve more than each alone by himself. We are much less afraid when we are two together. The chief condition of all spiritual

friendship is perfect frankness.   There is no better proof of true friendship than sincere reproof,
where such reproof is necessary.   We are occupied
in one great work, and in this consciousness all
that is small must necessarily disappear.

Ibid.

Why do we love so deeply?   Is not that also
God's will?   And if so why should that love ever
cease?   What should we be without it?   I cannot
believe that we are to surrender that love, that we
are to lose those who were given us to love.   Love
may be purified, may become more and more
unselfish, may be very different from what it was
on earth, but sympathy, suffering together and
rejoicing together, lies very deep at the root of all
being—were it ever to cease, our very being might
cease too.   We cannot help loving, loving more
and more, better and better.   Thus life becomes
brighter and brighter again, and we feel that we
have not lost those who are taken from us for a
little while.   We love them all the more, all the
better.   *MS.*

How selfish we are even in our love.   Here we
live for a short season, and we know we must part
sooner or later.   We wish to go first, and to leave

those whom we love behind us, and we sorrow because they went first and left us behind. As soon as one looks beyond this life, it seems so short, yet there was a time when it seemed endless.

MS.

The past is ours, and there we have all who loved us, and whom we love as much as ever, aye, more than ever.   *MS.*

MANKIND

THE earth was unintelligible to the ancients because looked upon as a solitary being, without a peer in the whole universe; but it assumed a new and true significance as soon as it rose before the eyes of man as one of many planets, all governed by the same laws, and all revolving around the same centre. It is the same with the human soul, and its nature stands before our mind in quite a different light since man has been taught to know and feel himself as a member of a great family—as one of the myriads of wandering stars all governed by the same laws, and all revolving around the same centre, and all deriving their light from the same source. "Universal History" has laid open new avenues of thought, and it has enriched our language with a word which never passed the lips of Socrates, or Plato, or Aristotle—*Mankind*. Where the Greek saw barbarians we see brethren; where the Greek saw nations, we see mankind, toiling and suffering, separated by oceans, divided by language, and severed by national enmity— yet evermore tending, under a Divine control, toward the fulfilment of that inscrutable purpose for which the world was created, and man placed in it, bearing the image of God. History therefore, with its dusty and mouldering pages, is to us as sacred a volume as the book of nature. In both we read, or we try to read, the reflex of the laws and thoughts of a Divine Wisdom. We believe that there is nothing irrational in either history or nature, and that the human mind is called upon to read and to revere in both the manifestations of a Divine Power.

Chips from a German Workshop.

There are two antagonistic schools—the one believing in a descending, the other in an ascending development of the human race; the one asserting that the history of the human mind begins of necessity with a state of purity and simplicity which gradually gives way to corruption, perversity, and savagery; the other maintaining that the first human beings could not have been more than one step above the animals, and that their whole history is one of progress toward higher perfection. With regard to the beginnings of religion, the one school holds to a primitive suspicion of something that is beyond—call it supernatural, transcendental, infinite, or divine. It considers a silent walking across this bridge of life, with eyes fixed on high, as a more perfect realisation of primitive religion

than singing of Vedic hymns, offering of Jewish
sacrifices, or the most elaborate creeds and articles.
The other begins with the purely animal and
passive nature of man, and tries to show how the
repeated impressions of the world in which he
lived drove him to fetichism and totemism, whatever these words may mean, to ancestor worship,
to a worship of nature, of trees and serpents, of
mountains and rivers, of clouds and meteors, of
sun and moon and stars, and the vault of heaven,
and at last to a belief in One who dwells in heaven
above.   *Ibid.*

MIND OR THOUGHT

WHEREVER we can see clearly, we see that what we call mind and thought consist in this, that man has the power not only to receive presentations like an animal, but to discover something general in them. This element he can eliminate and fix by vocal signs; and he can further classify single presentations under the same general concepts, and mark them by the same vocal signs. *Silesian Horseherd.*

Language and thought go hand in hand; where there is as yet no word, there is not yet an idea. The thinking capacity of the mind has its source in language, lives in language and develops continually in language. *Ibid.*

All our thoughts, even the apparently most abstract, have their natural beginnings in what passes daily before our senses. *Nihil in fide nisi quod ante fuerit in sensu.* Man may for a time be unheedful of these voices of nature; but they come

135

again and again, day after day, night after night, till at last they are heeded. And if once heeded, those voices disclose their purport more and more clearly, and what seemed at first a mere sunrise becomes in the end a visible revelation of the infinite, while the setting of the sun is transfigured into the first vision of immortality.   *Hibbert Lectures.*

As the evolution of nature can be studied with any hope of success in those products only which nature has left us, the evolution of mind also can be effectually studied in those products only which mind itself has left us. These mental products in their earliest form are always embodied in language, and it is in language, therefore, that we must study the problem of the origin, and of the successive stages in the growth of mind.   *Science of Thought.*

If language and reason are identical, or two names, or two aspects only of the same thing, and if we cannot doubt that language had an historical beginning and represents the work of man carried on through many thousands of years, we cannot avoid the conclusion that before those thousands

of years there was a time when the first stone of
the great temple of language was laid, and before
that time man was without language, and therefore
without reason.   *Ibid.*

MIRACLES

IF once the human mind has arrived at the conviction that *everything* must be accounted for, or, as it is sometimes expressed, that there is uniformity, that there is care and order in everything, and that an unbroken chain of cause and effect holds the whole universe together, then the idea of the miraculous arises, and we, weak human creatures, call what is not intelligible to us, what is not in accordance with law, what seems to break through the chain of cause and effect, a miracle. Every miracle, therefore, is of our own making, and of our own unmaking.   *Gifford Lectures, III.*

It is due to the psychological necessities of human nature, under the inspiring influence of religious enthusiasm, that so many of the true signs and wonders performed by the founders of religion have so often been exaggerated, and, in spite of the strongest protests of these founders themselves, degraded into mere jugglery. It is true that all this does not form an essential element of religion, as we now understand religion. Miracles are no

longer used as arguments in support of the
truth of religious doctrines. Miracles have
often been called helps to faith, but they
have so often proved stumbling blocks to
faith, and no one in our days would venture
to say that the truth as taught by any religion
must stand or fall by certain prodigious
events which may or may not have happened,
which may or may not have been rightly apprehended by the followers of Buddha, Christ, or
Mohammed.   *Gifford Lectures, II.*

Our Lord's ascension will have to be understood
as a sublime idea, materialised in the language of
children. Is not a real fact that happened in a
world in which nothing can happen against the
will of God, better than any miracle? Why should
we try to know more than we can know, if only we
firmly believe that Christ's immortal spirit ascended
to the Father? That alone is true immortality,
divine immortality; not the resuscitation of the
frail mortal body, but the immortality of the immortal divine soul. It was this rising of the Spirit,
and not of the body, without which, as St. Paul
said, our faith would be vain. It is the Spirit
that quickeneth, the flesh profiteth nothing.
                    Gifford Lectures, III.

It will be to many of the honest disciples of Christ a real day of Damascus when the very name of miracle shall be struck out of the dictionary of Christian theology. The facts remain exactly as they are, but the Spirit of truth will give them a higher meaning. What is wanted for this is not less, but more, faith, for it requires more faith to believe in Christ without than with the help of miracles. Nothing has produced so much distress of mind, so much intellectual dishonesty, so much scepticism, so much unbelief, as the miraculous element forced into Christianity from the earliest days. Nothing has so much impeded missionary work as the attempt to persuade people first not to believe in their own miracles, and then to make a belief in other miracles a condition of their becoming Christians. It is easy to say, "You are not a Christian if you do not believe in Christian miracles." I hope the time will come when we shall be told, "You are not a Christian if you cannot believe in Christ without the help of miracles." *Ibid.*

MUSIC

Music is the language of the soul, but it defies interpretation. It means something, but that something belongs not to this world of sense and logic, but to another world, quite real, though beyond all definition. . . . Is there not in music, and in music alone of all the arts, something that is not entirely of this earth ? . . . Whence comes melody ? Surely not from anything that we hear with our outward ears and are able to imitate, to improve, or to sublimise. . . . Here if anywhere we see the golden stairs on which angels descend from heaven and whisper sweet sounds into the ears of those who have ears to hear. Words cannot be so inspired, for words, we know, are of the earth, earthy. Melodies are not of the earth, and it is truly said: "Heard melodies are sweet, but those unheard are sweeter."

Auld Lang Syne.

NATURE

THERE is nothing so beautiful as being alone with nature; one sees how God's will is fulfilled in each bud and leaf that blooms and withers, and one learns to recognise how deeply rooted in one is this thirst for nature. In living with men one is only too easily torn from this real home; then one's own plans and wishes and fears spring up; then we fancy we can perfect something for ourselves alone, and think that everything must serve for our own ends and enjoyments, until the influence of nature in life, or the hand of God, arouses us, and warns us that we live and flourish not for enjoyment, nor for undisturbed quiet, but to bear fruit in another life.   *Life.*

When one stands amid the grandeur of nature, with one's own little murmurings and sufferings, and looks deep into this dumb soul, much becomes clear to one, and one is astounded at the false ideas one has formed of this life. It is but a short journey, and on a journey one can do without many things which generally seem necessary to us.

Yes, we can do without even what is dearest to our hearts, in this world, if we know that, after the journey we shall have to endure, we shall find again those who have arrived at the goal quicker and more easily than we have done. Now if life were looked upon as a journey for refreshment or amusement, which it ought not to be, we might feel sad if we have to make our way alone, but if we treat it as a serious business journey, then we know we have hard and unpleasant work before us, and enjoy all the more the beautiful resting places which God's love has provided for each of us in life.   *Ibid.*

In the early days of the world, the world was too full of wonders to require any other miracles. The whole world was a miracle and a revelation, there was no need for any special disclosure. At that time the heavens, the waters, the sun and moon, the stars of heaven, the showers and dew, the winds of God, fire and heat, winter and summer, ice and snow, nights and days, lightnings and clouds, the earth, the mountains and hills, the green things upon the earth, the wells, and seas and floods—all blessed the Lord, praised Him and magnified Him forever. Can we imagine a more powerful revelation? Is it for us to say that for the children of men to join in praising and magnifying Him who revealed Himself in His own way in all the magnificence, the wisdom and order of nature, is mere paganism, polytheism, pantheism, and abominable idolatry? I have heard many blasphemies; I have heard none greater than this.   *Gifford Lectures, II.*

OBSCURITY

THERE may be much depth of wisdom in all that darkness and vagueness, but I cannot help thinking that there is nothing that cannot be made clear, and bright, and simple, and that obscurity arises in all cases from slovenly thinking and lazy writing.   *MS.*

OLD AGE

SHARING the happiness of other people, entering into their feelings, living life over once more with them and in them, that is all that remains to old people. I suppose it was meant to be so, the principal object of life being the overcoming of self, in every sense of the word.   *Life.*

This is a lesson one has to learn as one grows older, to learn to be alone, and yet to feel one in spirit with all whom one loves, whether present or absent.   *MS.*

You cannot escape from old age, whether it comes slowly or suddenly, but it comes unawares, and you suddenly feel that you cannot walk or jump as you used to do, and even the muscles of the mind don't hold out as they used. Well, so it was meant to be, and it will be pleasant to begin again with new muscles, and to take up new work. After seeing a good deal of life, I still think the greatest satisfaction is work:

I do not mean drudgery, but one's own findings out.   *Life.*

    As one is getting old, and looks forward with fear rather than with hope to what is still in store for us, one learns to appreciate more and more the never failing pleasure of recalling all the bright and happy days that are gone. Gone they are, but they are not lost. Ever present to our calling and recalling, they assume at last a vividness such as they hardly had when present, and when we poor souls were trembling for every day and hour and minute that was going and ever going and would not and could not abide.

Ibid.

RELIGION AND RELIGIONS

God is not far from each one of those who seek God, if haply they may feel after Him. Let theologians pile up volume upon volume of what they call theology, religion is a very simple matter, and that which is so simple and yet so all-important to us, the living kernel of religion, can be found, I believe, in almost every creed, however much the husk may vary. And think what that means! It means that above and beneath and behind all religions there is one eternal, one universal religion, a religion to which every man belongs, or may belong. *Last Essays.*

True religion, that is, practical, active, living religion, has little or nothing to do with logical or metaphysical quibbles. Practical religion is life, is a new life, a life in the sight of God, and it springs from what may truly be called a new birth.
Ibid.

Our senses can never perceive a real boundary, be it on the largest or the smallest scale; they present to us everywhere the infinite as their background, and everything that has to do with religion has sprung out of this infinite background as its ultimate and deepest foundation.

Silesian Horseherd.

I cannot bring myself to take much interest in all the controversies that are going on [1865] in the Church of England. . . . No doubt the points at issue are great, and appeal to our hearts and minds, but the spirit in which they are treated seems to me so very small. How few men on either side give you the impression that they write face to face with God, and not face to face with men and the small powers that be. Surely this was not so in the early centuries, nor again at the time of the Reformation?   *Life.*

We live in two worlds: behind the seen is the unseen, around the Finite the Infinite, above the comprehensible the incomprehensible. There have been men who have lived in this world only, who seem never to have felt the real presence of the unseen: and yet they achieved some greatness as rulers of men, as poets, artists, philosophers, and discoverers. But the greatest among the great have done their greatest works in moments of self-forgetful ecstasy, in union and communion with a higher world: and when it was done, such was their silent rapture that they started back, and could not believe it was their own, their very own, and they ascribed the glory of it to God, by whatever name they called Him in their various utterances. And while the greatest among the great thus confessed that they were not of this world only, and that their best work was but in part their own, those whom we reverence as the founders of religions, and who were at once philosophers, poets, and rulers of men, called nothing their own, but professed to teach only either what their fathers had taught them, or what a far-off Voice had whispered in their ear. . . . The ancient religions were not founded like temples or palaces, they sprang up like sacred graves from the soil of humanity, quickened by the rays of celestial light. In India, Greece, Italy and Germany not even the names of the earliest prophets are preserved. And, if in other countries the forms and features of the authors of their religious faith and worship are still dimly visible amidst the clouds of legend and poetry, all of them, Moses as well as Zoroaster, Confucius, Buddha and Mohammed, seem to proclaim with one voice that their faith was no new faith, but the faith of their fathers; that their wisdom was not their own wisdom, but, like every good and perfect gift, given them from above. What should we learn from these prophets who from distant countries and bygone ages all bear the same witness to the same truth ? We should learn that though religions may be founded and fashioned into strange shapes by the hand of man, religion is one and eternal. From the first dawn that ever brightened a human hearth or warmed a human heart, one generation has told another that there is a world beyond the dawn; and the keynotes of all religion—the feeling of the Infinite, the bowing down before the incomprehensible, the yearning after the unseen—having once been set to vibrate, have never been altogether drowned in the strange and wild music of religious sects and sciences. The greatest prophets of the world have been those who at sundry times and in divers manners have proclaimed again and again in the simplest words the simple creed of the fathers, faith in the unseen, reverence for the incomprehensible, awe of the Infinite—or, simpler still love of God, and oneness with the All-Father.   *Ibid.*

I have endeavoured to make clear two things, which constitute the foundation of all religion: first that the world is rational, that it is the result of thought, and that in this sense only is it the creation of a being which possesses reason, or is reason itself (the *Logos*); and secondly that mind or thought cannot be the outcome of matter, but on the contrary is the *prius* of all things.　　*Silesian Horseherd.*

Religion is not philosophy; but there never has been a religion, and there never can be, which is not based on philosophy, and does not presuppose the philosophical notions of the people. The highest aim, toward which all philosophy strives, is and will always remain the idea of God, and it was this idea which Christianity grasped in the Platonic sense, and presented to us most clearly in its highest form, in the Fourth Gospel.　　*Ibid.*

There has been no entirely new religion since the beginning of the world. The elements and roots of religion were there, as far back as we can trace the history of man; and the history of religion shows us throughout a succession of new combinations of the same radical elements. An intuition of God, a sense of human weakness and dependence, a belief in a Divine government of the world, a distinction between good and evil, and a hope of a better life, these are some of the radical elements of all religions. Though sometimes hidden, they rise again and again to the surface. Though frequently distorted, they tend again and again to their perfect form. Unless they had formed part of the original dowry of the human soul, religion would have remained an impossibility, and the tongues of angels would have been to human ears but as sounding brass, or as tinkling cymbals. *Chips from a German Workshop.*

In lecturing on the origin and growth of religion, my chief object has been to show that a belief in God, in the immortality of the soul and in a future retribution, can be gained, and not only can be, but has been gained, by the right exercise of human reason alone, without the assistance of what has been called a special revelation. In doing this, I thought I was simply following in the footsteps of the greatest theologians of our time, and that I was serving the cause of true religion by showing, by ample historical evidence, gathered from the Sacred Books of the East, how what St. Paul, what the Fathers of the Church, what mediæval theologians, and what some of the most learned of modern divines had asserted again and again was most strikingly confirmed by the records of all non-Christian religions which have lately become accessible to us. I could not have believed it possible that, in undertaking this work, I should have exposed myself to attacks from theologians who profess and call themselves Christians, and who yet maintain that worst of all heresies, that during all the centuries that have elapsed and in all the countries of the world, God has left Himself without a witness, and has revealed Himself to one race only, the Jews of Palestine.   *Gifford Lectures, III.*

If there is one thing which a comparative study of religions places in the clearest light, it is the inevitable decay to which every religion is exposed. It may seem almost like a truism that no religion can continue to be what it was during the lifetime of its founders and its first apostles. Yet it is but seldom borne in mind that without constant reformation, i. e., without a constant return to its fountain head, every religion, even the most perfect, on account of its very perfection, more even than others—suffers from its contact with the world, as the purest air suffers from the mere fact of being breathed.

                    Chips from a German Workshop.

To each individual his own religion, if he really believes in it, is something quite inseparable from himself, something unique, that cannot be compared to anything else, or replaced by anything else. Our own religion is, in that respect, something like our own language. In its form it may be like other languages; in its essence, and in its relation to ourselves, it stands alone and admits of no peer or rival.   *Ibid.*

Three of the results to which, I believe, a comparative study of religion is sure to lead, I may here state:

1. We shall learn that religions, in their most ancient form, or in the minds of their authors, are generally free from many of the blemishes that attach to them in later times.

2. We shall learn that there is hardly one religion which does not contain some truth, some important truth; truth sufficient to enable those who seek the Lord and feel after Him, to find Him in their hour of need.

3. We shall learn to appreciate better than ever what we have in our own religion. No one who has not examined patiently and honestly the other religions of the world, can know what Christianity

really is, or can join with such truth and sincerity in the words of St. Paul, "I am not ashamed of the gospel of Christ."   *Ibid.*

Many are the advantages to be derived from a careful study of other religions, but the greatest of all is that it teaches us to appreciate more truly what we possess in our own. Let us see what other nations have had and still have in the place of religion, let us examine the prayers, the worship, the theology even of the most highly civilised races, and we shall then understand more thoroughly what blessings are vouchsafed to us in being allowed to breathe from the first breath of life the pure air of a land of Christian light and knowledge. We are too apt to take the greatest blessings as matters of course, and even religion forms no exception. We have done so little to gain our religion, we have suffered so little in the cause of truth, that however highly we prize our own Christianity, we never prize it highly enough until we have compared it with the religions of the rest of the world.   *Ibid.*

The spirit of truth is the life spring of all religion, and where it exists it must manifest itself, it must plead, it must persuade, it must convince and convert.   *Ibid.*

As there is a faculty of speech independent of all the historical forms of language, there is a faculty of faith in man, independent of all historical religions. If we say it is religion which distinguishes man from the animal, we do not mean the Christian and Jewish religion: we do not mean any special religion: but we mean a mental faculty or disposition, which, independent of, nay, in spite of, sense and reason, enables man to apprehend the Infinite under different names, and under varying disguises. Without that faculty, no religion, not even the lowest worship of idols and fetiches, would be possible; and if we will but listen attentively, we can hear in all religions a groaning of the spirit, a struggle to conceive the inconceivable, to utter the unutterable, a longing after the Infinite, a love of God.

Science of Religion.

Like an old precious metal, the ancient religion, after the dust of ages has been removed, will come out in all its purity and brightness; and the image which it discloses will be the image of the Father, the Father of all the nations upon earth;

and the superscription, where we can read it again, will be, not in Judæa only, but in the languages of all the races of the world, the Word of God revealed where alone it can be revealed—revealed in the heart of man.   *Ibid.*

If we granted that all religions, except Christianity and Mosaism, derived their origin from those faculties of the mind only which, according to Paley, are sufficient by themselves for calling into life the fundamental tenets of natural religion, the classification of Christianity and Judaism on one side as *revealed*, and of the other religions as *natural*, would still be defective, for the simple reason that no religion, though founded on revelation, can ever be entirely separated from natural religion. The tenets of natural religion, though they never constituted by themselves a real historical religion, supply the only ground on which even revealed religions can stand, the only soil where they can strike root, and from which they can receive nourishment and life.   *Ibid.*

The intention of religion, wherever we meet it, is always holy. However imperfect, however childish a religion may be, it always places the human soul in the presence of God: and however imperfect and however childish the conception of God may be, it always represents the highest ideal of perfection which the human soul, for the time being, can reach and grasp. Religion therefore places the human soul in the presence of its highest ideal, it lifts it above the level of ordinary goodness, and produces at last a yearning after a higher and better life—a life in the light of God.

Ibid.

I suppose that most of us, sooner or later in life, have felt how the whole world—this wicked world, as we call it—is changed as if by magic, if once we can make up our mind to give men credit for good motives, never to be suspicious, never to think evil, never to think ourselves better than our neighbours. Trust a man to be true and good, and, even if he is not, your trust will tend to make him true and good. It is the same with the religions of the world. Let us but once make up our minds to look in them for what is true and good, and we shall hardly know our old religions again. There is no religion—or, if there is, I do not know it—which does not say, "Do good, avoid evil." There is none which does not contain what Rabbi Hillel called the quintessence of all religions, the simple warning, "Be good, my boy." "Be good, my boy," may seem a very short catechism, but let us add to it, "Be good, my boy, for God's sake," and we have in it very nearly the whole of the Law and the Prophets.

Ibid.

In order to choose between different gods, and different forms of faith, a man must possess the faculty of choosing the instruments of testing truth and untruth, whether revealed or not; he must know that certain fundamental tenets cannot be absent in any true religion and that there are doctrines against which his rational or moral conscience revolts as incompatible with truth. In short, there must be the foundation of religion, there must be the solid rock, before it is possible to erect an altar, a temple, or a church: and if we call that foundation natural religion, it is clear that no revealed religion can be thought of which does not rest more or less firmly on natural religion.

Ibid.

Universal primeval revelation is only another name for natural religion, and it rests on no authority but the speculations of philosophers. The same class of philosophers, considering that language was too wonderful an achievement for the human mind, insisted on the necessity of admitting a universal primeval language, revealed directly by God to men, or rather to mute beings; while the more thoughtful and more reverent of the Fathers of the Church, and among the founders of modern philosophy also, pointed out that it was more consonant with the general working of an all-wise and all-powerful Creator that He should have endowed human nature with the essential conditions of speech instead of presenting mute beings with grammers and dictionaries ready-made. The same applies to religion. A universal primeval religion revealed direct by God to man, or rather to a crowd of atheists, may, to our human wisdom, seem the best solution of all difficulties; but a higher wisdom speaks to us out of the realities of history, and teaches us, if we will but learn, that "we have all to seek the Lord, if haply we may feel after Him, and find Him, though He is not far from every one of us."

Ibid.

The study of the ancient religions of mankind, I feel convinced, if carried on in a bold, but scholarlike, careful, and reverent spirit, will remove many doubts and difficulties which are due entirely to the narrowness of our religious horizon; it will enlarge our sympathies, it will raise our

thoughts above the small controversies of the day,
and at no distant future evoke in the very heart
of Christianity a fresh spirit and a new life.

Ibid.

No judge, if he had before him the worst of
criminals, would treat him as most historians and
theologians have treated the religions of the world..
Every act in the lives of their founders which
shows that they were but men, is eagerly seized
and judged without mercy; every doctrine that is
not carefully guarded is interpreted in the worst
sense that it will bear; every act of worship that
differs from our own way of serving God is held
up to ridicule and contempt. And this is not
done by accident but with a purpose, nay, with
something of that artificial sense of duty which
stimulates the counsel for the defence to see nothing
but an angel in his own client, and anything but
an angel in the plaintiff on the other side. The
result has been—as it could not be otherwise—a
complete miscarriage of justice, an utter misapprehension of the real character and purpose of
the ancient religions of mankind; and, as a
necessary consequence, a failure in discovering the
peculiar features which really distinguish Christianity from all the religions of the world, and
secure to its founder His own peculiar place in the

history of the world, far away from Zoroaster and
Buddha, from Moses and Mohammed, from
Confucius and Laotse. By unduly depreciating
all other religions, we have placed our own in a
position which its founder never intended for it;
we have torn it away from the sacred context of
the history of the world; we have ignored, or
wilfully narrowed, the sundry times and divers
manners in which, in times past, God spake unto
the fathers by the prophets; and instead of
recognising Christianity as coming in the fulness
of time, and as the fulfilment of the hopes and
desires of the whole world, we have brought
ourselves to look upon its advent as the only
broken link in that unbroken chain which is
rightly called the Divine government of the
world. Nay, worse than this, there are people
who, from mere ignorance of the ancient religions
of mankind, have adopted a doctrine more un-
christian than any that could be found in the
pages of the religious books of antiquity, i.e. that
all the nations of the earth, before the rise of
Christianity, were mere outcasts, forsaken and
forgotten of their Father in Heaven, without a
knowledge of God, without a hope of Heaven.
If a comparative study of the religions of the
world produced but this one result, that it drove
this godless heresy out of every Christian heart,

and made us see again in the whole history of the
world the eternal wisdom and love of God toward
all His creatures, it would have done a good work.

Ibid.

Do you still wonder at polytheism or at mythology? Why, they are inevitable. They are, if
you like, a *parler enfantin* of religion. But the
world has its childhood, and when it was a child,
it spoke as a child, it understood as a child, it
thought as a child, and in that it spoke as a child its
language was true. The fault rests with us, if
we insist on taking the language of children for
the language of men, if we attempt to translate
literally ancient into modern language, oriental
into occidental speech, poetry into prose.

Ibid.

Religion is inevitable if only we are left in
possession of our senses, such as we really find
them, not such as they have been defined for us.
We claim no special faculty, no special revelation.
The only faculty we claim is perception, the only
revelation we claim is history, or as it is now
called, historical evolution. But let it not be
supposed that we find the idea of the Infinite
ready made in the human mind from the very
beginning of our history. All we maintain is that

the germ or the possibility, the Not-yet of that
idea, lies hidden in the earliest sensuous perceptions, and that as reason is evolved from what is
finite, so faith is evolved from what from the
very beginning is infinite in the perceptions of our
senses.   *Hibbert Lectures.*

Each religion has its own peculiar growth, but
the seed from which they spring is everywhere the
same.   That seed is the perception of the Infinite,
from which no one can escape who does not wilfully
shut his eyes.   From the first flutter of human consciousness, that perception underlies all the other
perceptions of our senses, all our imaginings, all
our concepts, and every argument of our reason.
It may be buried for a time beneath the fragments
of our finite knowledge, but it is always there, and,
if we dig deep enough, we shall always find that
buried seed, supplying the living sap to the fibres
and feeders of all true faith.   *Ibid.*

Instead of approaching the religions of the world
with the preconceived idea that they are either
corruptions of the Jewish religion, or descended,
in common with the Jewish religion, from some
perfect primeval revelation, the students of the

science of religion have seen that it is their duty
first to collect all the evidence of the early history
of religious thought that is still accessible in the
sacred books of the world, or in the mythology,
customs, or even in the languages of various races.
Afterward they have undertaken a genealogical
classification of all the materials that have hitherto
been collected, and they have then only approached
the question of the origin of religion in a new spirit,
by trying to find out how the roots of the various
religions, the radical concepts which form their
foundation, and before all, the concept of the
Infinite, could have been developed, taking for
granted nothing but sensuous perception on one
side and the world by which we are surrounded
on the other.   *Ibid.*

A distinction has been made for us between
religion and philosophy, and, so far as form and
object are concerned, I do not deny that such a distinction may be useful.   But when we look to the
subjects with which religion is concerned, they are,
and always have been, the very subjects on which
philosophy has dwelt, nay, from which philosophy
has sprung.   If religion depends for its very life
on the sentiment or the perception of the Infinite
within the Finite and beyond the Finite, who is to

determine the legitimacy of that sentiment, or of that perception, if not the philosopher? Who is to determine the powers which man possesses for apprehending the Finite by his senses, for working up his single, and therefore finite, impressions into concepts by his reason, if not the philosopher? And who, if not the philosopher, is to find out whether man can claim the right of asserting the existence of the Infinite, in spite of the constant opposition of sense and reason, taking these words in their usual meaning? We should damnify religion if we separated it from philosophy: we should ruin philosophy if we divorced it from religion.   *Ibid.*

Who, if he is honest toward himself, could say that the religion of his manhood was the same as that of his childhood, or the religion of his old age the same as the religion of his manhood? It is easy to deceive ourselves, and to say that the most perfect faith is a childlike faith. Nothing can be truer, and the older we grow the more we learn to understand the wisdom of a childlike faith. But before we can learn that, we have first to learn another lesson, namely, to put away childish things. There is the same glow about the setting sun as there is about the rising sun; but there lies between the two a whole world, a journey through the whole sky, and over the whole earth.   *Ibid.*

I hope the time will come when the subterranean area of human religion will be rendered more and more accessible . . . and that the Science of Religion, which at present is but a desire and a seed, will in time become a fulfilment, a plenteous harvest. When that time of harvest has come, when the deepest foundations of all the religions of the world have been laid free and restored, who knows but that those very foundations may serve once more, like the catacombs, or like the crypts beneath our old cathedrals, as a place of refuge for those who, to whatever creed they may belong, long for something better, purer, older, and truer than what they can find in the statutable sacrifices, services and sermons of the days in which their lot on earth has been cast; some who have learnt to put away childish things, call them genealogies, legends, miracles, or oracles, but who cannot part with the childlike faith of their heart. Each believer may bring down with him into that quiet crypt what he values most, his own pearl of great price—the Hindu his innate disbelief in this world, his unhesitating belief in another world—the Buddhist his perception of an eternal law, his sub-

mission to it, his gentleness, his pity—the Mahom-
medan, if nothing else, his sobriety—the Jew his
clinging, through good and evil days, to the one
God, who loveth righteousness and whose name is
"I am"—the Christian that which is better than
all, if those who doubt it would only try it, our love
of God, call Him what you like, the Infinite, the
Invisible, the Immortal, the Father, the highest
Self, above all, and through all, and in all, manifested in our love of man, our love of the living,
our love of the dead, our living and undying love.

Ibid.

If we see the same doctrines, sometimes uttered
even in the very same words, by the Apostles, and
by what people call the false prophets of the
heathen world, we need not grudge them these
precious pearls.   When two religions say the same
thing, it is not always the same thing, but even if it
is, should we not rather rejoice and try with all our
might to add to what may be called the heavenly
dowry of the human race, the common stock of
truth which, as we are told, is not far from every
one of us, if only we feel after it and find it.

Gifford Lectures, I.

Religion, when looked upon not as supernatural,
but as thoroughly natural to man, has assumed a

new meaning and a higher dignity when studied as an integral part of that historical evolution which has made man what he is, and what from the very first he was meant to be. Is it no comfort to know that at no time and in no part of the world, has God left Himself without witness, that the hand of God was nowhere beyond the reach of the outstretched hands of babes and sucklings; nay, that it was from those rude utterances out of the mouths of babes and sucklings, that is, of savages and barbarians, that has been perfected in time the true praise of God? To have looked for growth and evolution in history as well as in nature is no blame, and has proved no loss to the present or to the last century; and if the veil has as yet been but little withdrawn from the Holy of Holies, those who come after us will have learnt at least this one lesson, that this lifting of the veil which was supposed to be the privilege of priests, is no longer considered as a sacrilege, if attempted by any honest seekers after truth.   *Ibid.*

Religion consists in the perception of the Infinite under such manifestations as are able to influence the moral character of man,   *Ibid.*

No opinion is true simply because it has been held either by the greatest intellects or by the largest number of human beings at different periods in the history of the world. No one can spend years in the study of the religions of the world, beginning with the lowest and ending with the highest forms, no one can watch the sincerity of religious endeavour, the warmth of religious feeling, the nobleness of religious conduct, among races whom we are inclined to call pagan or savage, without learning at all events a lesson of humility. Anybody, be he Jew, Christian, Mohammedan, or Brahmin, if he has a spark of modesty left, must feel that it would be nothing short of a miracle that his own religion alone should be perfect throughout, while that of every other believer should be false or wrong from beginning to end.   *Ibid.*

The more we study the history of the religions of the world, the clearer it becomes that there is really no religion which could be called an individual religion, in the sense of a religion created, as it were *de novo*, or rather *ab ovo*, by one single person. This may seem strange, and yet it is really most natural. Religion, like language, is everywhere an historical growth, and to invent a completely new religion would be as hopeless a task as to invent a completely new language. Nor do the founders of the great historical religions of the world ever claim this exclusive authorship. On the contrary, most of them disclaim in the strongest terms the idea that they have come either to destroy or to build a completely new temple.   *Ibid.*

The whole world in its wonderful history has passed through the struggle for life, the struggle for eternal life; and every one of us, in his own not less wonderful history, has had to pass through the same wonderful struggle: for, without it, no religion, whatever its sacred books may be, will find in the human heart that soil in which alone it can strike root and on which alone it can grow and bear fruit. We must all have our own bookless religion, if the Sacred Books, whatever they may be, are to find a safe and solid foundation within ourselves. No temple can stand without that foundation, and it is because that foundation is so often neglected that the walls of the temple become unsafe and threaten to fall.   *Ibid.*

The heart and mind and soul of man are the same under every sky, in all the varying circumstances of human life; and it would be awful to believe that *any* human beings should have been deprived of that light "which lighteth every man that cometh into the world." It is that light which lighteth *every* man, and which has lighted all the religions of the world, call them bookless or literate, human or divine, natural or supernatural, which alone can dispel the darkness of doubt and fear that has come over the world. What our age wants more than anything else is *Natural Religion.* Whatever meaning different theologians may attach to *Supernatural Religion,* history teaches us that nothing is so natural as the supernatural. But the supernatural must always be *superimposed* on the natural. Supernatural religion without natural religion is a house built on sand, and when, as in our days, the rain of doubt descends, and the floods of criticism come, and the winds of unbelief and despair blow, and beat upon that house, that house will fall because it was not founded on the rock of bookless religion, of natural religion, of eternal religion.

Ibid.

Every religion, being the property of the young and the old, the wise and the foolish, must always be a kind of compromise, and, while protesting against real corruptions and degradations, we must learn to bear with those whose language differs from our own, and trust that in spite of the tares which have sprung up during the night, some grains of wheat will ripen toward the harvest in every honest heart. *Gifford Lectures, II.*

In all the fundamentals of religion we are neither better nor worse than our neighbours, neither more wise nor more unwise than all the members of that great family who have been taught to know themselves as children of one and the same Father in Heaven. *Ibid.*

What can a study of Natural Religion teach us? Why, it teaches us that religion is natural, is real, is inevitable, is universal. Is that nothing? Is it nothing to know that there is a solid rock on which all religion, call it natural or supernatural, is founded? Is it nothing to learn from the annals of history that God has not left Himself without witness in that He did good, and gave us rain from heaven and fruitful seasons, filling our hearts, and the hearts of the whole human race, with food and gladness?" *Ibid.*

While on the one side a study of Natural Religion teaches us that much of what we are inclined to class as natural, to accept as a matter of course, is in reality full of meaning, is full of God, is in fact truly miraculous, it also opens our eyes to another fact, namely that many things we are inclined to class as supernatural are in reality perfectly natural, perfectly intelligible, nay, inevitable, in the growth of every religion.   *Ibid.*

The real coincidences between all the religions of the world teach us that all religions spring from the same soil—the human heart—that they all look to the same ideals, and that they are all surrounded by the same dangers and difficulties. Much that is represented to us as supernatural in the annals of the ancient religions of the world becomes perfectly natural from this point of view.   *Ibid.*

To those who see no difficulties in their own religion, the study of other religions will create no new difficulties. It will only help them to appreciate more fully what they already possess. For with all that I have said in order to show that other religions also contain all that is necessary for salvation, it would be simply dishonest on my part were I to hide my conviction that the religion taught by Christ, free as yet from all ecclesiastical fences and

intrenchments, is the best, the purest, the truest
religion the world has ever seen.   *Ibid.*

To expect that religion could ever be placed
again beyond the reach of scientific treatment or
honest criticism, shows an utter misapprehension
of the signs of the times, and would, after all, be
no more than to set up private judgment against
private judgment. If the inalienable rights of
private judgment, that is, of honesty and truth,
were more generally recognised, the character of
religious controversy would at once be changed.
It is restriction that provokes resentment, and
thus embitters all discussions on religious
subjects.   *Gifford Lectures, III.*

So far from being dishonest, the distinction
between a higher and a lower form of religion is
in truth the only honest recognition of the realities of life. If to a philosophic mind religion is
a spiritual love of God and the joy of his full
consciousness of the spirit of God within him,
what meaning can such words convey to the
millions of human beings who nevertheless want
a religion, a positive, authoritative, or revealed
religion, to teach them that there is a God, and

that His commands must be obeyed without questioning ?   *Ibid.*

People ask what can be gained by a compre-
hensive study of religions, by showing that, as
yet, no race has been discovered without some
word for what is not visible, not finite, not human,
for something superhuman and divine. Some
theologians go even so far as to resent the discovery of the universality of such a belief. They
are anxious to prove that human reason alone
could never have arrived at a conception of God.
They would much rather believe that God has
left Himself without witness than that a belief
in something higher than the Finite could spring
up in the human heart from gratitude to Him
who gave us rain from heaven, and fruitful seasons,
filling our hearts with food and gladness. *Ibid.*

Physical religion, beginning in a belief in agents
behind the great phenomena of nature, reached
its highest point when it had led the human mind
to a belief in one Supreme Agent or God, whatever His name might be. It was supposed that
this God could be implored by prayers and pleased
by sacrifices. He was called the Father of gods

and men. Yet even in His highest conception
He was no more than what Cardinal Newman
defined God to be. "I mean by the Supreme
Being," he wrote, "one who is simply self-depend-
ent, and the only being who is such. I mean that
He created all things out of nothing, and could
destroy them as easily as He made them, and that,
in consequence, He is separated from them by an
abyss, and incommunicable in all His attributes."
This abyss separating God from man remains at
the end of Physical Religion. It constitutes its
inherent weakness. But this very weakness becomes in time a source of strength, for from it
sprang a yearning for better things. Even the
God of the Jews, in His unapproachable majesty,
though He might be revered and loved by man
during his life on earth, could receive as it were
a temporary allegiance only, for "the dead cannot
praise God, neither any that go down into darkness!" God was immortal, a man was mortal;
and Physical Religion could not throw a bridge
over the abyss that separated the two. Real
religion, however, requires more than a belief in
God; it requires a belief in man also, and an
intimate relation between God and man, at all
events in a life to come. There is in man an
irrepressible desire for continued existence. It
shows itself in life in what we may call self defence.

It shows itself at the end of life and at the approach
of death, in the hope of immortality.   *Ibid.*

So long as we look on the history of the human
race as something that might or might not have
been, we cannot wonder that the student of
religion should prefer to form his opinions of the
nature of religion and the laws of its growth from
the masterpiece of Thomas Aquinas, the "Summa
Sacra Theologiæ," rather than from the "Sacred
Books of the East." But when we have
learned to recognise in history the realisation
of a rational purpose, when we have learnt
to look upon it as in the truest sense of the
word a Divine Drama, the plot revealed in
it ought to assume in the eyes of a philosopher
also a meaning and a value far beyond the
speculations of even the most enlightened and
logical theologians.   *Gifford Lectures, IV.*

The question is whether there is, or whether
there is not, hidden in every one of the sacred
books, something that could lift up the human
heart from this earth to a higher world, something that could make man feel the omnipresence
of a higher Power, something that could make

him shrink from evil and incline to good,
something to sustain him in the short journey through life, with its bright moments
of happiness, and its long hours of terrible
distress.   *Preface to Sacred Books of the East.*

It has been truly said, and most emphatically,
by Doctor Newman, that neither a belief in God
by itself, nor a belief in the soul by itself, would
constitute religion, and that real religion is founded
on a true perception of the relation of the soul to
God, and of God to the soul.

Gifford Lectures, IV.

It may be truly said that the founders of the
religions of the world have all been bridge builders.
As soon as the existence of a beyond, of a Heaven
above the earth, of Powers above us and beneath
us, had been recognised, a great gulf seemed to
be fixed between what was called by various
names, the earthly and the heavenly, the material
and the spiritual, the phenomenal and noumenal,
or best of all, the visible and invisible world, and it
was the chief object of religion to unite these two
worlds again, whether by the arches of hope and
fear, or by the iron chains of logical syllogisms.

Ibid.

Religion, in order to be *real* religion, a man's own religion, must be searched for, must be discovered, must be conquered. If it is simply inherited, or accepted as a matter of course, it often happens that in later years it falls away, and has either to be reconquered, or to be replaced by another religion.   *Autobiography.*

Religion is growth, never finished. From the lowest to the highest stages it is growth, not willed only, nor given only, but both. The lowest stages may seem very imperfect to us, but they are all the more important. Language and mythology show us the old path on which man travelled from Nature to God.   *MS.*

There is no lesson which at the present time seems more important than to learn that in every religion there are precious grains: that we must draw in every religion a broad distinction between what is essential and what is not, between the eternal and the temporary, between the divine and the human, and that though the non-essential may fill many volumes, the essential can often be comprehended in a few words, but words on which "hang all the law and the prophets."

Preface to Sacred Books of the East.

Religions were meant to be many like languages. To us one language for the whole human race would seem to be far better; but it was not to be. Each language was to be a school for each race, a talent committed to each nation. And so it is with religion. There is truth in all of them, the whole truth in none. Let each one cherish his own, purify his own, and throw away what is dead and decaying. But to give up one's religion is like giving up one's life. Even the lowest savage must keep his own old faith in God, when he becomes converted to Christianity, or he will have lost the living and life-giving root of his faith. If people would only learn to look for what is good in all religions, how far more beautiful the world would appear in their eyes. They dig hard enough to get the ore from out a mine, they sift it, smelt it, purify it, and then keep the small pieces of gold they have got with all this trouble, forgetting the *scoriæ* and all the refuse. That is what we must do as students of religion—but we do the very contrary, we hug the *scoriæ* and shut our eyes to the glittering rays of gold. Jews and

Christians are worse in that respect than all other people. It may be because their religions are freer from human impurities than all other religions. But why should that make them blind to what is really good in other religions; why should it blind them so much that they look upon other religions as the work of the Devil? The power of evil has had its work in all religions, our own not excepted—but the power of goodness prevails everywhere. Till we know that, life and history seem intolerable. It would not put an end to missionary labour; it would only make it more a labour of love, less painful to those whom we wish to win, not away from their God, but back to their God, Him whom they ignorantly worship, and whom we should declare unto them —according to our own light, such as it is, less dark than theirs on many points, but yet dark, as those know best who, like St. Paul, have striven hardest to look through the glass of our own weak human mind.   *MS.*

If people would only learn to see that there is really a religion beyond all religions, that each man must have his own religion which he has conquered for himself, and that we must learn to tolerate religion wherever we find it. Christianity would be a perfect religion, if it did not go beyond the simple words of Christ, and if, even in these words, we made full allowance for the time and place and circumstances in which they were spoken, that is, if we simply followed Christ where He wishes us to follow Him. We have gone far beyond those times and circumstances in many things, but in what is most essential we are still far behind the teaching of Christ. How many call themselves Christians who have no idea how difficult it is to be a Christian, a follower of Christ. It is easy enough to repeat creeds, and to work ourselves into a frame of mind when miracles seem most easy. *MS.*

It was the duty of the Apostles and of the early Christians in general to stand forth in the name of the only true God, and to prove to the world that their God had nothing in common with the idols worshipped at Athens and Ephesus. It was the duty of the early converts to forswear all allegiance to their former deities, and if they could not at once bring themselves to believe that the gods whom they had worshipped had no existence at all, they were naturally led on to ascribe to them a kind of demoniacal nature, and to curse them as the offspring of that new principle of Evil with which they had become acquainted in the doctrines of the early Church. . . . Through the whole of St. Augustine's works, and through all the works of earlier Christian divines, there runs the same spirit of hostility blinding them to all that may be good, and true, and sacred, and magnifying all that is bad, false, and corrupt, in the ancient religions of mankind. Only the Apostles and their immediate disciples venture to speak in a different, and, no doubt, in a more truly Christian spirit, of the old forms of worship. . . . What can be more convincing, more powerful, than the language of St. Paul at Athens? *Science of Language.*

Those who believe that there is a God, and that He created heaven and earth, and that He ruleth the world by His unceasing providence, cannot believe that millions of human beings, all created like ourselves in the image of God, were, in their time of ignorance, so utterly abandoned that their whole religion was falsehood, their whole worship a farce, their whole life a mockery. An honest and independent study of the religions of the world will teach us that it was not so . . . that there is no religion which does not contain some grains of truth. Nay, it will teach us more;

it will teach us to see in the history of the ancient religions, more clearly than anywhere else, the *Divine education of the human race.* *Ibid.*

    The Divine, if it is to reveal itself at all to us, will best reveal itself in our own human form. However far the human may be from the Divine, nothing on earth is nearer to God than man, nothing on earth more godlike than man. And as man grows from childhood to old age, the idea of the Divine must grow with us from the cradle to the grave, from grace to grace. A religion which is not able thus to grow and live with us as we grow and live is dead already. Definite and unvarying uniformity, so far from being a sign of honesty and life, is always a sign of dishonesty and death. Every religion, if it is to be a bond between the wise and the foolish, the old and the young, must be pliant, must be high and deep and broad; bearing all things, believing all things, hoping all things, enduring all things. The more it is so the greater its vitality, the greater the strength and warmth of its embrace.

Hibbert Lectures.

REVELATION

TRUE inspiration is, and always has been, the spirit of truth within, and this is but another name for the spirit of God. It is truth that makes inspiration, not inspiration that makes truth. Whoever knows what truth is knows also what inspiration is: not only *theopneustos*, blown into the soul by God, but the very voice of God, the real presence of God, the only presence in which we, as human beings, can ever perceive Him.

Autobiography.

There is nothing in the idea of revelation that excludes progress, for whatever definition of revelation we may adopt, it always represents a communication between the Divine on one side and the Human on the other. Let us grant that the Divine element in revelation, that is, whatever of truth there is in revelation, is immutable, yet the human element, the recipient, must always be liable to the accidents and infirmities of human nature. That human element can never be eliminated in any religion. . . . To ignore that human element in all religions is like ignoring

187

the eye as the recipient and determinant of the
colours of light.　We know more of the sun than
our forefathers, though the same sun shone on
them that shines on us;　and if astronomy has
benefited by its telescopes . . . theology also
ought not to despise whatever can strengthen the
farsightedness of human reason in its endeavour
to gain a truer and purer idea of the Divine.　A
veil will always remain.　But as in every other
pursuit, so in religion also, we want less and less
of darkness, more and more of light;　we want,
call it life, or growth, or development, or progress;
we do not want mere rest, mere stagnation, mere
death.　　　　　　　　　　　　*Gifford Lectures, I.*

It was the sense of an overpowering truth which
led to the admission of a revelation.　But while
in the beginning truth made revelation, it soon
came to pass that revelation was supposed to
make truth.　When we see this happening in every
part of the world, when we can watch the psychological progress which leads in the most natural
way to a belief in supernatural inspiration, it will
hardly be said that an historical study of religion
may be useful to the antiquarian, but cannot help
us to solve the burning questions of the day.

Ibid.

I believe in one revelation only—the revelation within us, which is much better than any revelations which come from without. Why should we look for God and listen for His voice outside us only, and not within us? Where is the temple of God, or the true kingdom of God? *Life.*

There are Christian mystics who would not place internal revelation, or the voice of God within the heart, so far below external revelation. To those who know the presence of God within the heart, this revelation is far more real than any other can be. They hold with St. Paul that man is in the full sense of the word the temple of God, and that the Spirit of God dwelleth within him; nay, they go even further, and both as Christians and as mystics they cling to the belief that all men are one in the Father and the Son, as the Father is in the Son, and the Son in the Father. There is no conflict in their minds between Christian doctrine and mystic doctrine. They are one and the same in character, the one imparted through Christ on earth, the other imparted through the indwelling spirit of God, which again is Christ, as born within us. The Gospel of St. John is full of passages to which the Christian mystic clings, and by which he justifies his belief in the indwelling spirit of God, or as he also calls it, the birth of Christ in the human soul.

Gifford Lectures, II.

I cannot connect any meaning with a primeval revelation, or with an original knowledge of God. A knowledge of God is surely at all times impossible; man can only trust, he cannot know. He can feel the Infinite, and the Divine, he can never class it or subdue it by knowledge. The question seems to me, how our unconscious relation to God, which must be there and can never be destroyed, becomes gradually more and more conscious, and that is what one can best learn to understand in the history of the various religions of the world— so many voyages of discovery, each full of sufferings and heroic feats, all looking toward the same Pole, each to be judged by itself, none, I believe, to be condemned altogether.   *MS.*

To assume that every word, every letter, every parable, every figure was whispered to the authors of the Gospels, is certainly an absurdity, and rests only on human . . . authority. But the true revelation, the real truth, as it was already anticipated by the Greek philosophers, slowly accepted by Jews, like Philo and the contemporaries of Jesus, taught by men like Clement and Origen in the ancient Greek Church, and, in fine, realised in the life of Jesus, and sealed by His death, is no absurdity: it is for every thinking Christian the eternal life, or the Kingdom of God on earth, which Jesus wished to establish, and in part did establish.   To become a citizen of this Kingdom is the highest that man can attain, but it is not attained merely through baptism and confirmation; it must be gained in earnest spiritual conflict.   *Silesian Horseherd.*

THE RIG-VEDA

THE Veda alone of all works I know treats of a genesis of God-consciousness, compared to which the Theogony of Hesiod is like a wornout creature. We see it grow slowly and gradually with all its contradictions, its sudden terrors, its amazements, and its triumphs. As God reveals His Being in Nature in her order, her indestructibility, in the eternal victory of light over darkness, of spring over winter, in the eternally returning course of the sun and the stars, so man has gradually spelt out of nature the Being of God, and after trying a thousand names for God in vain we find Him in the Veda already saying: "They call him Indra, Mitra, Varuna; then they call him the Heavenly, the bird with beautiful wings; that which is One they call in various ways." . . . The belief in immortality is only the other side, as it were, of the God-consciousness, and both are originally natural to the Aryan race. *Life*.

SCIENCE

EVERY true Science is like a hardy Alpine guide that leads us on from the narrow, through it may be the more peaceful and charming valleys of our preconceived opinions, to higher points, apparently less attractive, nay, often disappointing for a time, till, after hours of patient and silent climbing, we look round, and see a new world around us.   *Chips from a German Workshop.*

A new horizon has opened, our eyes see far and wide, and as the world beneath us grows wider and larger, our own hearts seem to grow wider and larger, and we learn to embrace the far and distant, and all that before seemed strange and indifferent, with a warmer recognition and a deeper human sympathy; we form wider concepts, we perceive higher truths.   *Ibid.*

What is natural is divine, what is supernatural is human.   *Gifford Lectures, I.*

Man is the measurer of all things, and what is Science but the reflection of the outer world on the mirror of the mind, growing more perfect, more orderly, more definite, more great, with every generation? To attempt to study nature without studying man is as impossible as to study light without studying the eye. I have no misgivings, therefore, that the lines on which this College [Mason Science College] is founded will ever become so narrow as to exclude the science of man, and the science of that which makes man, the science of language, and, what is really the same, the science of thought. And where can we study the science of thought, that most wonderful instance of development, except in the languages and literatures of the past? How are we to do justice to our ancestors except by letting them plead their own case in their own language? Literary culture can far better dispense with physical science than physical science with literary culture, though nothing is more satisfactory than a perfect combination of the two. *Life.*

THE SELF

As behind the various gods of nature, one supreme deity was at last discovered in India; the Brahmans imagined that they perceived behind the different manifestations of feeling, thought, and will also, a supreme power which they called Atma, or Self, and of which the intellectual powers or faculties were but the outward manifestations. This led to a philosophy which took the place of religion, and recognised in the Self the only true being, the unborn and therefore immortal element in man. A step further led to the recognition of the original identity of the subjective Self in man, and the objective Self in nature, and thus, from an Indian point of view, to a solution of all the riddles of the world. The first commandment of all philosophy, " Know thyself," became in the philosophy of the Upanishads, "Know thyself as the Self," or, if we translate it into religious language, "Know that we live and move and have our being in God."

Gifford Lectures, I.

The death of a child is as if the flash of the Divine eye had turned quickly away from the

mirror of this world, before the human consciousness woke up and thought it recognised itself in
the mirror, often only to perceive for a moment,
just as it closes its eyes for the last time, that that
which it took for itself was the shadow or reflection
of its eternal Self.   *Life.*

A man need not go into a cave because he has
found his true Self; he may live and act like every-
body else; he is "living but free." All remains
just the same, except the sense of unchangeable,
imperishable self which lifts him above the
phenomenal self. He knows he is wearing clothes,
that is all. If a man does not see it, if some of his
clothes stick to him like his very skin, if he fears
he might lose his identity by not being a male
instead of a female, by not being English instead
of German, by not being a child instead of a man,
he must wait and work on. Good works lead to
quietness of mind, and quietness of mind to true
self knowledge. Is it so very little to be only
Self, to be the subject that can resist, i. e.,
perceive the whole universe, and turn it into
his object? Can we wish for more than
what we are, lookers on—resisting what tries to
crush us, call it force, or evil, or anything else?
                                                 Ibid.

The impression made on me by the look of a child who is not yet conscious of himself and of the world round him, is that of still undisturbed godliness.   Only when self-consciousness wakes little by little, through pleasure or pain, when the spirit accustoms itself to its bodily covering, when man begins to say *I* and the world to call things *his*, then the full separation of the human self from the Divine begins, and it is only after long struggles that the light of *true* self-consciousness sooner or later breaks through the clouds of earthly semblances, and makes us again like the little children "of whom is the Kingdom of Heaven."   In God we live and move and have our being; that is the sum of all human wisdom, and he who does not find it here will find it in another life. All else that we learn on earth, be it the history of nature or of mankind, is for this end alone, to show us everywhere the presence of a Divine providence, and to lead us through the knowledge of the history of the human spirit to the knowledge of ourselves, and through the knowledge of the laws of nature to the understanding of that human nature to which we are subjected in life.

Ibid.

To my mind the birth of a child is not a breach of the law of continuity, but on that very ground

I must admit the previous existence of the Self that is here born as a child, and which brings with it into this new order of things simply its self-consciousness, and even that not developed but undeveloped potentia, in a sleep. When afterward a child awakes to self-consciousness, that is really its remembrance of its former existence. The Self which it becomes conscious of, remember, is in its essence not of this world only, but of a former as well as of a future world. This constitutes in fact the only distinct remembrance in every human being of a former life. There are besides indistinct remembrances of his former existence, viz., the many dispositions which every thinking man finds in himself, and which are not simply the result of the impressions of this world on a so-called *tabula rasa*. Unless we begin life as *tabula rasa* we begin it as *tabula preparata*, as *leukomata*, and whatever colour or disposition, or talent, or temperament, whatever there is inexplicable in each individual, that he will perceive, or possibly remember, as the result of the continuity between his present and former life.   *MS.*

What then is that which we call Death ? Separation of the Self from a living body. If so, does

the body die because the Self leaves it, or does the
Self leave the body because it dies? What has
life to do with the Self? Has the Self which for
a time dwells in a living body anything to do with
what we call the life of that body? Does the Self
take possession of a body because it lives, or does
the body live because the Self has taken possession
of it? The difficulty arises from our vague conception of *life*. Life is only a mode of existence.
Existence is possible without what we call
life, not life without existence. To live means
to be able to absorb, but who or what is
able? The Self exists, it is sentient, capable
of perception by becoming embodied. It is
perceptive because sentient, it is conceptive
because perceptive. The difficulty lies in the
embodiment. It is there where all philosophy
becomes ridiculous. *MS*.

Knowledge belongs to the Self alone, call it
what we will. The nerve fibres might vibrate as
often as they pleased, millions and millions of
times in a second; they could never produce the
sensation of red if there were no Self as the receiver
and illuminator, the translator of these vibrations
of ether; this Self that alone receives, alone
illumines, alone knows, and of which we can say

nothing more than that it exists, that it perceives, and as the Indian philosophers add, that it is blessed, i. e., that it is complete in itself, serene and eternal.   *Silesian Horseherd.*

SORROW AND SUFFERING

How mysterious all this suffering is, particularly when it produces such prostration that it must lose all that elevating power which one knows suffering does exercise in many cases. It seems sometimes as if a large debt of suffering had to be paid off, and that some are chosen to pay a large, very large, sum so that others may go free. We have our own burden to bear, but it is a burden that seems to make other things easy to bear—it strengthens even when it seems to crush. But how could one bear that complete prostration of all powers which must make death seem so much preferable to life. And yet life goes on, and people care about a hundred little things, and break their hearts if they do not get them. *MS.*

Such trials as you have had to pass through are not sent without a purpose, and if you say that they have changed your views of life, such a change in a character like yours can only be a change in advance, a firmer faith in those truths which have been revealed to the dim sight of human nature, a stronger will to resist all falsehood and tampering with the truth, and a deeper conviction that we owe our life to Him who has given it, and that we must fight His battle when He calls us to do it.   *MS.*

God knows that we want rain and storm as much as sunshine, and He sends us both as seems best to His love and wisdom. When all breaks down He lifts us up. But when we feel quite crushed and forsaken and alone, we then feel the real presence of our truest Friend, who whether by joys or sorrows, is always calling us to Him, and leading us to that true Home where we shall find Him, and in Him all we loved, with Him all we believed, and through Him all we hoped for and aspired to on earth. Our broken hearts are the truest earnest of everlasting life.   *Life.*

We must submit, but we must feel it a great blessing to be able to submit, to be able to trust that infinite love which embraces us on all sides, which speaks to us through every flower and every worm, which always shows us beauty and per- fection, which never mars, never destroys, never wastes, never deceives, never mocks.   *MS.*

There is but one help and one comfort in these trials, that is to know by whom they are sent.   If one knows that nothing can happen to us without Him, one does not feel quite helpless, even under the greatest terrors of this life.   *MS.*

How little one thinks that many trials and afflictions may come upon us any day.   One lives as if life were to last forever, and as if we should never part with those who are most dear to us. Life would be intolerable were it otherwise, but how little one is prepared for what life really is.
                                    MS.

Why is there so much suffering in this world? I cannot think it improves us much, and yet it must have its purpose.   All these are questions far too high for us—we are like children and more than children, when we come to think of them. All we know is that where we catch a glimpse of God's handiwork, either in the natural or moral world, it is so wonderfully perfect, so beyond all our measures, that we feel safe as in a good ship, however rough the sea may be.   Whatever we may believe or hope, or wish for, will be far exceeded by that Higher Will and Wisdom which supports all, even us little souls.   *MS.*

The sorrows of life are inevitable, but they are hard to bear, for all that. They would be harder still if we did not see their purpose of reminding us that our true life is not here, but that we are here on a voyage that may be calm or stormy, and which is to teach us what all sailors have to learn, courage, perseverance, kindness, and in the end complete trust in a Higher Power.   *MS.*

Sorrow is necessary and good for men; one learns to understand that each joy must be indemnified by suffering, that each new tie which knits our hearts to this life must be loosed again, and the tighter and the closer it was knit, the keener the pain of loosening it. Should we then attach our hearts to nothing, and pass quietly and unsympathetically through this world, as if we had nothing to do with it? We neither could nor ought to act so. Nature itself knits the first tie between parents and children, and new ties through our whole life. We are not here for reward, for the enjoyment of undisturbed peace or from mere accident, but for trial, for improvement, perhaps for punishment; for the only union which can secure the happiness of men, the union between our Self and God's Self, is broken, or at least obscured, by our birth, and the highest object of our life is to find this bond again, to remain ever conscious of it and hold fast to it in life and in death. This rediscovery of the eternal union between God and man constitutes true religion among all people. *Life.*

Everyone carries a grave of lost hope in his soul, but he covers it over with cold marble, or with green boughs. On sad days one likes to go alone to this God's acre of the soul, and weep there, but only in order to return full of comfort and hope to those who are left to us. *Ibid.*

The sorrows of life, like all other things, pass away, and the larger the number who await us beyond, the easier the parting from those we leave behind. *Ibid.*

Grief is a sweet remembrance of happiness that was. *MS.*

There is the old riddle always before me, why was —— taken from me? Human understanding has no answer for it, and yet I feel as certain as I can feel of anything that as it is, it is good, it is best, better than anything I can wish for. One feels one's own ignorance why what seems so right and natural should not be, and yet one knows it could not be. One hides one's head in the arms of a Higher Power, a Friend, a Father, and more than a Father. Wait, and you will know. Work, and you will be able to bear it.   *MS.*

People think that grief is pain, but it is not so: Grief, the absorption in the quiet recollection of what was, but is no longer, is a pleasure, a consolation, a blessing.   *MS.*

Those who would comfort us by bidding us forget our grief, and join their happy gatherings, do not know what comfort is. Hearts which have suffered have a right to what the world may call grief and sorrow, but what is really a quiet communion with those whom we love, and whom we can find no longer among the laughter of the happy.   *MS.*

What can we pray for? Not for special gifts, but only for God's mercy. We do not know what is good for us, and for others. What would become of the world if all our prayers were granted? And yet it is good to pray—that is, to live in all our joys and sorrows, with God, that unknown God whom we cannot reason with but whom we can love and trust. Human misery, outward and inward, is certainly a great problem, and yet one knows from one's own life how just the heaviest burdens have been blessings. The soul must be furrowed if it is to bear fruit. *MS.*

What is the tenure of all our happiness? Are we not altogether at the mercy of God? Would it not be fearful to live for one day unless we knew, and saw, and felt His Presence and Wisdom and Love encompassing us on all sides? If we once feel that, then even death, even the death of those we love best and who love us best, loses much of its terror: it is part and parcel of one great system of which we see but a small portion here, and which without death, without that bridge of which we see here but the first arch, would seem to be a mere mockery. That is why I said to you it is well that human art cannot prolong our life forever, and in that sentiment I should think we both agree. I have felt much for you, more than I cared to say. We are trained differently, but we are all trained for some good purpose, and the suffering which you

have undergone is to me like deep ploughing, the
promise of a rich harvest.   *Life.*

There is a large and secret brotherhood in this
world, the members of which easily recognise each
other, without any visible outward sign.   It is the
band of mourners.   The members of this brotherhood need not necessarily wear mourning; they can
even rejoice with the joyful and they seldom sigh
or weep when others see them.   But they recognise
and understand each other, without uttering a word,
like tired wanderers, who, climbing a steep moun-
tain, overtake other tired wanderers, and pause,
and then silently go on again, knowing that they all
hope to see the same glorious sunset high up above.
Their countenances reflect a soft moonlight; when
they speak, one thinks of the whispering of the leaves
of a beech forest after a warm spring shower, and
as the rays of the sun light up the drops of dew
with a thousand colours, and drink them up from
the green grass, a heavenly light seems to shine
through the tears of the mourners, to lighten them
and lovingly kiss them away.   Almost everyone,
sooner or later, enters this brotherhood, and those
who enter it early may be considered fortunate,
for they learn, before it is too late, that *all* which
man calls his own is only lent him for a short time,

and the ivy of their affections does not cling so deeply and so strongly to the old walls of earthly happiness.   *Ibid.*

   We cannot know, we cannot name the Divine, nor can we understand its ways as manifested in nature and human life.   We ask why there should be suffering and sin, we cannot answer the question. All we can say is, it is willed to be so.   Some help our human understanding may find, however, by simply imagining what would have been our life if the power of evil had not been given us.   It seems to me that in that case we, human beings as we are, should never have had a conception of what is meant by good: we should have been like the birds in the air, happier, it may be, but better, no.   Or if suffering had always been reserved for the bad, we should all have become the most cunning angels.   Often when I am met by a difficulty which seems insoluble, I try that experiment, and say, Let us see what would happen if it were otherwise.   Still, I confess there is some suffering on earth which goes beyond all understanding, which even the truest Christian love and charity seems unable to remove or mitigate.   It can teach us one thing only, that we are blind, and that in the darkness of the night we lose our faith in a dawn which will drive away darkness, fear and despair. Much, no doubt, could be done even by what is now communism, but what in earlier days was called Christianity. And then one wonders whether the world can ever again become truly Christian. I dare not call myself a Christian. I have hardly met the man in all my life who deserved that name. Again, I say, let us do our best, knowing all the time that our best is a mere nothing.

Ibid.

THE SOUL

THE name of the immortal element (in man) was not given to man as a gratuitous gift. It had to be gained, like the name of God, in the sweat of his face. Before man could say that he believed his soul to be immortal, he had to discover that there was a soul in man. It required as great an effort to form such a word as *anima*, breath, and to make it signify the infinite in man, as to form such a word as *diva*, bright, and to make it signify the infinite in nature.   *Gifford Lectures, III.*

To us the two words "body" and "soul" are so familiar that it seems almost childish to ask how man came at first to speak of body and soul. But what did he mean by soul? What do we ourselves mean by soul? Think of the many meanings contained in our word soul. Our soul may mean the living soul; it may mean the sentient soul; it may mean the seat of the passions whether good or bad; it may mean the organ of thought; and lastly, the immortal element in man. The question we have to ask is not, how man arrived at a name

for soul, but how he came for the first time to speak
of something different from the body.   *Ibid.*

The discovery of the soul, the first attempts at
naming the soul, started everywhere from the simplest observations of material facts. The lesson cannot be inculcated too often that the whole wealth
of our most abstract and spiritual words comes
from a small number of material or concrete terms.
                                                      Ibid.

We see that the way which led to the discovery
of a soul was pointed out to man as clearly as was
the way which led him to the discovery of the gods.
It was chiefly the breath, which almost visibly left
the body at the time of death, that suggested the
name of breath, and afterward the thought of
something breathing, living, perceiving, willing,
remembering, and thinking within us.   The name
came first, the name of the material breath.   By
dropping what seemed material even in this airy
breath, there remained the first vague and airy
concept of what we call soul.   *Ibid.*

The worship of the spirits of the departed which,
under various forms, was so widely spread over

the ancient world, could not but accustom the human mind to the idea that there was something in man which deserved such worship. The souls of the departed were lifted higher and higher, till at last they reached the highest stage which existed in the human mind, namely that of divine beings, in the ancient sense of that word. *Ibid.*

The problem of uniting the invisible and visible worlds presented itself under three principal aspects. The first was the problem of creation, or how the invisible Primal Cause could ever come in contact with visible matter and impart to it form and meaning. The second problem was the relation between God and the individual soul. The third problem was the return of the soul from the visible to the invisible world, from the prison of its mortal body to the freedom of a heavenly paradise. The individual soul as dwelling in a material body forms part of the created world, and the question of the return of the soul to God is therefore closely connected with that of its creation by, or its emanation from, God.

Gifford Lectures, IV.

When the original oneness of earth and heaven, of the human and the divine natures, has once been discovered, the question of the return of the soul to God assumes a new character. It is no longer a question of an ascension to heaven, an approach to the throne of God, an ecstatic vision of God, and a life in a heavenly Paradise. The vision of God is rather the knowledge of the divine element in the soul, and of the consubstantiality of the divine and human natures. Immortality has no longer to be asserted, because there can be no death for what is divine and therefore immortal in man. There is life eternal and peace eternal for all who feel the divine Spirit as dwelling within them, and have thus become the children of God.   *Ibid.*

No doubt the soul must find it difficult in childhood to accustom itself to the human body, and it takes many years before it is quite at home. Then for a time all goes well, and the soul hardly knows it is hidden in a strange garment till the body begins to be weakly, and can no longer do all the soul wishes, and presses it everywhere, so that the soul appears to lose all outward freedom and movement. Then one can well understand that we long to be gone, and death is a true deliverance. God always knows best when the right time comes.

Life.

Let us remember that we do not know what the soul was before this life—nay, even what it was during the first years of our childhood. Yet we believe on very fair evidence that what we call our soul existed from the moment of our birth. What ground have we, then, to doubt that it was even before that moment? To ascribe to the soul a beginning on our birthday would be the same as to claim for it an end on the day of our death, for whatever has a beginning has an end. If then in the absence of any other means of knowledge, we may take refuge in analogy, might we not say that it will be with the soul hereafter as it has been here, and that the soul after its earthly setting will rise again, much as it rose here? This is not a syllogism; it is analogy, and in a cosmos like ours analogy has a right to claim some weight, in the absence of any proof to the contrary. *Last Essays.*

There is a question which has probably been asked by every human heart: "Granting that the soul cannot, without self-contradiction, be mortal, will that soul be itself, know itself, and will it know others whom it has known before?" For the next life, it is said, would not be worth living if the soul did not recollect itself, recognise not only itself, but those whom it has known and

loved on earth.   Here analogy alone can supply
some kind of answer: "It will be hereafter as it
has been" is not, in the absence of any evidence
to the contrary, an argument that can be treated
with contempt.   Our soul here may be said to
have risen without any recollection of itself and
of the circumstances of its former existence.   But
it has within it the consciousness of its eternity,
and the conception of a beginning is as impossible
for it as that of an end, and if souls were to meet
again hereafter as they met in this life, as they
loved in this life, without knowing that they had
met and loved before, would the next life be so
very different from what this life has been here on
earth—would it be so utterly intolerable and
really not worth living ?   *Ibid*.

When the soul has once reached that union
with God, nay, when it lives in the constant presence of God, evil becomes almost impossible.
We know that most of the evil deeds to which
human nature is prone are possible in the dark
only.   Before the eyes of another human being,
more particularly of a beloved being, they become
at once impossible.   How much more in the real
presence of a real and really beloved God, as felt
by the true mystic, not merely as a phrase, but as

a fact? As long as there is no veil between him and God, evil thoughts, evil words, and evil deeds are simply impossible to one who feels the actual presence of God. Nor is he troubled any longer by questions, such as how the world was created, how evil came into the world. He is satisfied with the Divine Love that embraces his soul; he has all that he can desire, his whole life is hid through Christ in God, death is swallowed up in victory, the mortal has become immortal, neither death nor life, nor things present, nor things to come, is able to separate his soul from the love of God. *Gifford Lectures, IV.*

THEOSOPHY

THIS venerable name (Theosophy) so well known among early Christian thinkers, as expressing the highest conception of God within the reach of the human mind, has of late been so greatly misappropriated that it is high time to restore it to its proper function. It should be known once for all that one may call oneself a theosophist without . . . believing in any occult sciences and black art.

Gifford Lectures, IV.

There is nothing esoteric in Buddhism. Buddhism is the very opposite of esoteric—it is a religion for the people at large, for the poor, the suffering, the ill-treated. Buddha protests against the very idea of keeping anything secret. There was much more of that esoteric teaching in Brahmanism. There was the system of caste, which deprived the Sudras, at least, of many religious privileges. But I do say that even in Brahmanism there is *no such thing as an esoteric interpretation of the Sastras.* The Sastras have but one meaning, and all who had been properly prepared by education

had access to them. There are some artificial
poems, which are so written as to admit of two
interpretations. They are very wonderful, but
they have nothing to do with philosophical doctrines. Again there are erotic poems in Sanscrit
which are explained as celebrating the love and
union between the soul and God. But all this is
perfectly well known, there is no mystery in it.

Life.

TRUTH

WHAT is wanted is the power of sifting evidence, and a simple love of truth. Whatever value we may attach to our own most cherished convictions there is something more cherished than all of them, and that is a perfect trust in truth, if once we have seen it.   *Last Essays.*

True reverence does not consist in declaring a subject, because it is dear to us, to be unfit for free and honest inquiry; far from it! True reverence is shown in treating every subject, however sacred, however dear to us, with perfect confidence, without fear and without favour; with tenderness and love, by all means, but, before all, with unflinching and uncompromising loyalty to truth.   *Science of Religion.*

Do we lose anything if we find that what we hold to be the most valuable truth is shared in and supported by millions of human beings? Ancien philosophers were most anxious to support their own belief in God by the unanimous testimony of mankind. They made the greatest efforts to prove that there was no race so degraded and barbarous as to be without a belief in something divine. Some modern theologians seem to grudge to all religions but their own the credit of having a pure and true, nay, any concept of God at all, quite forgetful of the fact that a truth does not cease to be a truth because it is accepted universally. I know no heresy more dangerous to true religion than this denial that a true concept of God is within the reach of every human being, is, in fact, the common inheritance of mankind, however fearfully it may have been misused and profaned by Christian and un-Christian nations.

Gifford Lectures, II.

If Comparative Theology has taught us anything, it has taught us that there is a common fund of truth in all religions, derived from a revelation that was neither confined to one nation, nor miraculous in the usual sense of that word, and that even minute coincidences between the doctrines, nay, between the external accessories of various religions, need not be accounted for at once by disguised borrowings, but can be explained by other and more natural causes.

Ibid.

Can there be anything higher and better than truth? Is any kind of religion possible without an unquestioning trust in truth? No one knows what it is to believe who has not learnt to believe in truth, for the sake of truth, and for the sake of truth only.   *Gifford Lectures, III.*

It may be quite right to guard against dangers, whether real or imaginary, so long as it is possible. But when it is no longer possible, the right thing is to face an enemy bravely. Very often the enemy will turn out a friend in disguise. We cannot be far wrong, if we are only quite honest, but if we are once not quite honest over a few things, we shall soon become dishonest over many things.   In teaching on religion, even on Natural Religion, we must look neither right nor left, but look all facts straight in the face to see whether they are facts or not, and, if they are facts, to find out what they mean.   *Ibid.*

Some people say that they can derive no help, no comfort, from what they call spiritual *only.* Spiritual *only*—think what that *only* would mean, if it could have any meaning at all. We might as well say of light that it is light only, and that what we want is the shadow which we can grasp. So long as we know the shadow only, and not the light that throws it, the shadow only is real, and not the light. But when we have once turned our head and seen the light, the light only is real and substantial, and not the shadow.   *Ibid.*

We find in the Upanishads what has occupied the thoughts of man at all times, what occupies them now and will occupy them forever—a search after truth, a desire to discover the Eternal that underlies the Ephemeral, a longing to find in the human heart the assurance of a future life, and an attempt to reunite the bond which once held the human and the divine together, the true atonement between God and man.   *Ibid.*

We have toiled for many years and been troubled with many questionings, but what is the end of it all? We must learn to become simple again like little children. That is all we have a right to be: for this life was meant to be the childhood of our souls, and the more we try to be what we were meant to be, the better for us. Let us use the powers of our minds with the greatest freedom and love of truth, but let us never forget that we are, as Newton said, like children playing on the seashore, while the great ocean of truth lies undiscovered before us.   *Life.*

Nothing I like better than when I meet a man who differs from me; he always gives me something, and for that I am grateful.   Nor am I at all so hopeless as many people, who imagine that two people who differ can never arrive at a mutual understanding. . . . Why do people differ, considering that they all begin with the same love of truth and are all influenced by the same environment ?   Well, they often differ because one is ignorant of facts which the other knows and has specially studied. . . . But in most cases people differ because they use their words loosely, and because they mix up different subjects instead of treating them one by one.   *Ibid.*

THE WILL OF GOD

THROUGH my whole life I have learned this one lesson—that nothing can happen to us, unless it be the will of God. There can be no disappointment in life if we but learn to submit our will to the will of God. Let us wait for a little while, and to those whose eyes are turned to God and eternity the longest life is but a little while—let us wait, then, in faith, hope, and charity; these three abide, but the greatest of these is charity.   *Life*.

Whatever happens to us is always the best for us, even if we do not at once understand and perceive it.   *MS*.

Surely everything is ordered, and ordered for our true interests. It would be fearful to think that anything, however small in appearance, could happen to us without the will of God. If you admit the idea of chance or unmeaning events anywhere, the whole organisation of our life in

God is broken to pieces. We are, we don't know where, unless we rest in God and give Him praise for all things. We must trust in Him whether He sends us joy or sorrow. If He sends us joy, let us be careful. Happiness is often sent to try us, and is by no means a proof of our having deserved it. Nor is sorrow always a sign of God's displeasure, but frequently, nay, always, of His love and compassion. We must each interpret our life as best we can, but we must be sure that its deepest purpose is to bring us back to God through Christ. Death is a condition of our life on earth; it brings the creature back to its Creator. The creature groans at the sight of death, but God will not forsake us at the last, He who has never forsaken us from the first breath of our life on earth. If it is His will we may live to serve Him here on earth for many happy years to come. If He takes either of us away, His name be praised. We live in the shadow of death, but that shadow should not darken the brightness of our life. It is the shadow of the hand of our God and Father and the earnest of a higher, brighter life hereafter. Our Father in Heaven loves us more than any husband can love his wife, or any mother her child. His hand can never hurt us, so let us hope and trust always. *Life.*

Our lives are in the hands of a Father who knows what is best for all of us. Death is painful to the creature, but in God there is no death, no dying; dying belongs to life, and is only a passage to a more perfect world into which we all go when God calls us. When one's happiness is perfect, then the thought of death often frightens one, but even that is conquered by the feeling and the faith that all is best as it is, and that God loves us more than even a father and mother can love us. It is a beautiful world in which we live, but it is only beautiful and only really our home when we feel the nearness of God at each moment and lean on Him and trust in His love. . . . When the hour of parting comes, we know that love never dies and that God who bound us closely together in this life will bring us together where there is no more parting. *MS.*

WONDER

THERE are few sensations more pleasant than that of wondering. We have all experienced it in childhood, in youth, in manhood, and we may hope that even in our old age this affection of the mind will not entirely pass away. If we analyse this feeling of wonder carefully, we shall find that it consists of two elements. What we mean by wondering is not only that we are startled or stunned—that I should call the merely passive element of wonder. When we say "I wonder," we confess that we are taken aback, but there is a secret satisfaction mixed up with our feeling of surprise, a kind of hope, nay, almost of certainty, that sooner or later the wonder will cease, that our senses or our mind will recover, will grapple with these novel expressions or experiences, grasp them, it may be, know them, and finally triumph over them. In fact, we wonder at the riddles of nature, whether animate or inanimate, with a firm conviction that there is a solution to them all, even though we ourselves may not be able to find it. Wonder, no doubt, arises from ignorance, but from a peculiar kind of ignorance, from what might be called a fertile ignorance; an ignorance which, if we look back at the history of most of our sciences, will be found to have been the mother of all human knowledge.

Chips from a German Workshop.

WORDS

WHAT people call "mere words" are in truth the monuments of the fiercest intellectual battles, triumphant arches of the grandest victories won by the intellect of man. When man had formed names for body and soul, for father and mother, and not till then, did the first art of human history begin. Not till there were names for right and wrong, for God and man, could there be anything worthy of the name of human society. Every new word was a discovery, and these early discoveries, if but properly understood, are more important to us than the greatest conquests of the kings of Egypt and Babylon. Not one of our greatest explorers has unearthed more splendid palaces than the etymologist. Every word is the palace of a human thought, and in scientific etymology we possess the charm with which to call these ancient thoughts back to life.

Chips from a German Workshop.

Cannot a concept exist without a word? Certainly not, though in order to meet every possible objection we may say that no concept can exist without a sign, whether it be a word or anything else. And if it is asked whether the concept exists first and the sign comes afterward, I should say No: the two are simultaneous, but in strict logic the sign, being the condition of a concept, may really be said to come first. After a time, words may be dropped, and it is then, when we try to remember the old word that gave birth to our concept, that we are led to imagine that concepts came first and words afterward. I know how difficult it is to see this clearly. We are so accustomed to think without words that we can hardly realise the fact that originally no conceptual thought was possible without these or other signs.

Gifford Lectures, I.

WORK

IF you have found a work to which you are ready to sacrifice the whole of your life, and if you have faith in yourselves, others will have faith in you, and, sooner or later, a work that must be done will be done.   *Gifford Lectures, II.*

What flimsy things the so-called pleasures of life are—how little in them that lasts. To delight in doing one's work is life—that is what helps us on, though the road is sometimes very stiff and tiring—uphill rather, it would seem, than downhill, and yet downhill it is.   *MS.*

A distaste for work is only another name for a distaste for duty, a disregard for those commandments which hold society together, a disregard of the commandments of God. No doubt there is that reward in work that after a time it ceases to be distasteful, and like many a bitter medicine becomes liked, but that reward is vouchsafed to honest work only.   *MS.*

232

Work is the best healer of sorrow. In grief or disappointment try hard work; it will not fail you.
Autobiography.

No sensible man ought to care about posthumous praise, or posthumous blame. Enough for the day is the evil thereof. Our contemporaries are our right judges, our peers have to give their votes in the great academies and learned societies, and if they on the whole are not dissatisfied with the little we have done, often under far greater difficulties than the world was aware of, why should we care for the distant future? *Ibid.*

Put your whole heart, or your whole love into your work. Half-hearted work is really worse than no work. *Last Essays.*

Much of the best work in the world is done by those whose names remain unknown, who work because life's greatest bliss is work, and who require no reward beyond the consciousness that they have enlarged the knowledge of mankind and contributed their share to the final triumph of honesty and truth.
Chips from a German Workshop.

True immortality (of fame) is the immortality of the work done by man, which nothing can make undone, which lives, works on, grows on forever. It is good to *ourselves* to remember and honour the names of our ancestors and benefactors, but to them, depend upon it, the highest reward was not the hope of fame, but their faith in themselves, their faith in their work, their faith that nothing really good can ever perish, and that Right and Reason must in the end prevail.   *Ibid.*

It is given to few scholars only to be allowed to devote the whole of their time and labour to the one subject in which they feel the deepest interest. We have all to fight the battle of life before we can hope to secure a quiet cell in which to work in the cause of learning and truth.   *Ibid.*

What author has ever said the last word he wanted to say, and who has not had to close his eyes before he could write *finis* to his work?

Autobiography.

THE WORLD

THERE is no other Christian explanation of the world than that God thought and uttered it, and that man follows in life and thought the thoughts of God. We must not forget that all our knowledge and hold of the world are again nothing but thoughts, which we transform under the law of causality into objective realities. It was this unswerving dependence on God in thought and life that made Jesus what He was, and what we should be if we only tried, viz.: children of God.

Silesian Horseherd.

I cannot help seeing order, law, reason or *Logos* in the world, and I cannot account for it by merely *ex post* events, call them what you like—survival of the fittest, natural selection, or anything else.

Last Essays.

Think only what it was to believe in an order of the world, though it be no more at first than a belief that the sun will never overstep his bounds. It was all the difference between a chaos and a cosmos, between the blind play of chance and an

intelligible and therefore an intelligent providence.
How many souls, even now when everything else
has failed them, when they have parted with the
most cherished convictions of their childhood,
when their faith in man has been poisoned, and
when the apparent triumph of all that is selfish,
ignoble, and hideous has made them throw up
the cause of truth, of righteousness and innocence
as no longer worth fighting for, at least in this
world; how many, I say, have found their last
peace and comfort in the contemplation of the
order of the world, whether manifested in the
unvarying movement of the stars, or revealed in
the unvarying number of the petals and stamens
and pistils of the smallest forget-me-not. How
many have felt that to belong to this cosmos, to
this beautiful order of nature, is something at
least to rest on, something to trust, something to
believe, when everything else has failed. To us,
this perception of law and order in the world may
seem very little, but to the ancient dwellers on
earth, who had little else to support them, it was
everything—because, if once perceived, if once
understood, it could never be taken from them.

Hibbert Lectures.

We must learn to see a meaning in everything.
No doubt we cannot always see cause and effect,